PRAISE FOR L(

T0276665

"Michele Sullivan's beautiful book shows us that cultivating empathy and compassion for others can bring out the best in us. Her message is much needed at a time when so much human progress depends on connection and understanding."

—Sheryl Sandberg, COO of Facebook and founder of LeanIn.org and OptionB.org

"This woman is a health hazard for bores or anyone crying into their beer . . . unless they're tears of laughter or joy. She's so sharp you could cut yourself on these pages. Michele has the brain of a neurophysicist and a spirit the size of the sky. If you want to be uplifted, Look this book Up."

—Bono, musician and philanthropist

"Michele Sullivan has spent a lifetime dismantling assumptions and challenging traditional points of view—about both people and organizations. The lessons from *Looking Up* in her career in philanthropy show the power of both individual leadership and collaborative partnership."

—Michael Bloomberg, founder of Bloomberg LP and Bloomberg Philanthropies and three-term mayor of New York City

"*Looking Up* is an uplifting memoir about the journey of an inspiring woman who saw no limits despite being born with a rare form of dwarfism. Throughout this book, Michele takes you on her personal journey that makes you laugh and cry as she refuses to be defined by what some would call a 'disability.' After reading *Looking Up*, you would be hard-pressed to see Michele as disabled at all—rather, she is differently abled. She is pure grace and grit, a unique combination enabling her to overcome all obstacles to successfully accomplish her personal and professional goals, some of which we might think are well beyond our own limits."

—Cynthia DiBartolo, founder, chairwoman, and CEO of Tigress Financial Partners

"This book is a helpful resource for anyone interested in personal and professional growth. Because you are in charge of your own growth, I'd encourage you to grab a copy and read it with your team. I'm certainly going to do just that!"

—Clay Scroggins, author of *How to Lead in a World of Distraction*

"Be inspired to look up when your instinct may be to turn away. This book elicits a call to change perspective, to view people as they truly are and not only what we see. By changing her own perspective, Michele has changed the lives of millions of people around the globe. An inspiring read for all!"

—Scott Harrison, founder and CEO of charity: water
and author of *Thirst: A Story of Redemption, Compassion,
and a Mission to Bring Clean Water to the World*

"Throughout my career I was influenced and touched by some amazing leaders—Michele is one of them. As I strived to be a better leader, I learned from the example she set by embracing diversity and practicing the principles she has outlined in *Looking Up*. As I have dealt with the challenges of an ALS diagnosis, I have drawn from the courage Michele demonstrates each and every day. Her book will make you laugh and cry but more importantly, think. Enjoy."

—Ed Rapp, former Caterpillar Group president

"Michele's call to action is simple but profound: strip away the deep-seated biases and view others, instead, for their inherent value. Her captivating story and the enlightened lessons woven within will inspire you to live better, and to elevate others along your path."

—Bill Kurtis, award-winning journalist

"When we look up to others, we discover their true value and it places an indelible imprint on our lives. Investing, both financially and emotionally, in social impact endeavors will not only improve our businesses, families, and communities—it will make us better people. Valuing those around us and giving of ourselves are essential and less complicated than you may think. Within these pages, Michele will inspire you, call you to action, and impart genuine wisdom."

—Jeff Whiteman, president/CEO of Empire Southwest

LOOKING UP

LOOKING UP

How a Different Perspective Turns
Obstacles into Advantages

MICHELE L.
SULLIVAN

HARPERCOLLINS
LEADERSHIP

AN IMPRINT OF HARPERCOLLINS

Published by HarperCollins Leadership, an imprint of HarperCollins Focus LLC.

Any internet addresses, phone numbers, or company or product information printed in this book are offered as a resource and are not intended in any way to be or to imply an endorsement by HarperCollins Leadership, nor does HarperCollins Leadership vouch for the existence, content, or services of these sites, phone numbers, companies, or products beyond the life of this book.

Scripture quotations marked NIV are taken from the Holy Bible, New International Version®, NIV®. Copyright © 1973, 1978, 1984, 2011 by Biblica, Inc.™ Used by permission of Zondervan. All rights reserved worldwide. www.zondervan.com. The "NIV"and "New International Version" are trademarks registered in the United States Patent and Trademark Office by Biblica, Inc.™

Photograph of author with Barack Obama courtesy of the White House. All other photos courtesy of the author and used with permission.

ISBN 978-1-4002-1441-9
ISBN 978-1-4002-1432-7 (eBook)
ISBN 978-1-4002-1431-0 (HC)

Library of Congress Cataloging-in-Publication Data

Names: Sullivan, Michele, 1965- author.
Title: Looking up : how a different perspective turns obstacles into advantages / Michele Sullivan.
Description: [Nashville. TN] : HarperCollins Leadership, an imprint of HarperCollins Focus LLC, [2020] | Includes bibliographical references. | Summary: "Michele Sullivan, who has a rare form of dwarfism, shares how her physical posture taught her the most effective relational posture with others, which helped her become one of the most powerful women in philanthropy"-- Provided by publisher.
Identifiers: LCCN 2019031474 | ISBN 9781400214310 (hardcover) | ISBN 9781400214327 (ebook)
Subjects: LCSH: Attitude change. | Interpersonal communication. | Vulnerability (Personality trait)
Classification: LCC HM1186 .S85 2020 | DDC 303.3/8--dc23
LC record available at https://lccn.loc.gov/2019031474

This book is dedicated to my family and to those who choose every day to look up to others instead of down on them.

CONTENTS

FOREWORD

H i, Cherie—I'm Michele Sullivan." This is how our
friendship began in 2014, with a perfect blend of warmth
and poise, as I'm sure it has for many others who have been
lucky enough to meet Michele. We got on from the start and
I felt inspired by the introduction. We met while attending
the annual United Nations General Assembly (UNGA),
where there are endless esteemed and accomplished people
to meet. Michele and I instantly found a common ground:
we were both there to elevate others. Michele was there with
the Caterpillar Foundation, and I was representing the work
of the Cherie Blair Foundation for Women and the incredible
women entrepreneurs I have the privilege of working with all
over the world.

I started the foundation in 2008, with the vision of working toward economic equality between men and women, and
we've been incredibly successful, helping nearly 150,000 aspir-
ing women entrepreneurs across the world to start and grow
businesses. Michele's work with the Caterpillar Foundation

had caught my attention in the months prior to attending the UNGA. I told Michele how I was a fan of her work. It was true then and it remains so today.

Our friendship has grown over the years since we first met. We've found that the pair of us share important values: we both have a deep commitment to the rights of women, of children, and of those across the world who are unseen, overlooked, or unjustly disadvantaged. Moreover, whilst our lives have been different in so many ways, we also have shared experiences of making our way as women in the world—and we are far from alone. Women like Marisol Márquez, who was a participant in my foundation's flagship entrepreneurship program and runs a production company in Mexico, are often at the sharp end of discrimination. Marisol has to take her male partner with her to business meetings to be taken seriously. As a young woman making her way in the world, a man must be sitting next to her to legitimize her voice.

Although, of course, all of our experiences are unique and some of us are far luckier than others, Michele, Marisol, and I share this sense of familiarity with pushing back against discrimination and inequity with millions of others—men, women, and children—across the world. This has fundamentally shaped the course of our lives.

In this book, you will find a woman whose story, though different in detail from mine and yours, is our story. We all have inherent value. And we have all been misunderstood and misrepresented at certain points in our lives. We've all been overlooked and underestimated more than once or twice, and it's so often women who experience this most acutely. Michele's story is a tribute to overcoming adversity with grace and strength, and is a timely reminder of the change we can all make in the world.

This book poses important questions for us to consider: Will we seek to see the true value in others, whether or not they see value in us? Will we advocate for others, even if they don't or can't advocate for us? I encourage you to consider your answers as you turn the coming pages. I believe that if more of us embraced Michele's message, and lived it with true conviction, we could make profound changes to the world around us.

Cherie Blair CBE, QC

Leading Queen's Counsel, committed campaigner for women's rights, wife of the former British prime minister, and founder of the Cherie Blair Foundation for Women
May 10, 2019

INTRODUCTION

The Long and Short of It

I'm sure you picked up this book wondering what a little person might teach you. Honestly, I'd wonder the same thing if I saw someone like me on the cover. I'm also sure you're coming to this book with some curiosity about the life I've led . . . what it's like being small in a world where size and stature seem to really matter . . . what other people do when they see me or what I do when I see them seeing me. You might even wonder whether I drive a car or how I high-five or where I buy my clothes. Don't feel bad about any of that. I have curiosities about you too.

Our brains are hardwired to wonder about the people we see and then make quick conclusions about them before we've met. We walk into a room, and our brains immediately take account of who and what is in it. At a glance, we determine all kinds of things. Who's safe and who's not. Who we can learn from and who we can't. Who's like us and who isn't. My brain still does this today, even though assumptions have been thrust upon me my entire life. No matter what others have assumed about you, your brain still assumes about others too.

Even if we know the swift conclusions we form are arbitrary, and many have been proven wrong before, we still carry a powerful, natural affection for the instincts we're counting on to survive in the world. We have to learn to override this instinct by remembering that surviving isn't the point of life. Thriving is. This requires embracing a broader perspective on others instead of the snap judgments our brains form at first glance.

If you're older than seven, you're probably taller than me. Ironically, always being the shorter one has given me some legitimate advantages. For starters, my shorter vantage point has forced me to look up to others my entire life. While it can be intimidating, even today, this permanent physical posture has taught me that the most powerful relational posture I can have with others is to look up to them rather than down on them.

Learning to expand my view of others has been the most potent lesson in my life. It was the reason I didn't choose the life of obscurity that some disabled persons feel is their only option, homebound and relegated to a handful of safe relationships with people who don't stare. An expanded perspective on others is also the reason I was able to pursue my dreams, despite my disabilities, and land at the helm of one of the world's most prominent philanthropic organizations, responsible for investing tens of millions of dollars every year in worthy causes. In short, how I've learned to see the people around me—to always look up to them rather than down on them—is the foundation of my leadership; it's given my life its greatest impact and meaning. But this isn't just my lesson. I believe looking up to others is the foundation of all human progress. Period. Can you imagine how the world would change if we all began looking up to each other?

When we learn how to elevate the people around us, to discover and champion what's noble and beautiful and powerful in them, we uncover the path of impact in one another's lives. Others can teach us, even (and often more so) if they are different. We can affirm them, even if *we* are different. I hope my story illuminates this powerful dynamic and the profound lessons I've found within it. I can't offer you any more than my experience. And there's no guarantee that my words will reach your head or your heart. I wish I could say everything in person, sitting down somewhere together, talking face-to-face—I'll sit on twelve inches of cushions. Since we can't do that yet, I hope I can at least get you thinking bigger about the impact you can have when you learn how to look up to the people around you, whoever they are, wherever they're from, whatever they look like.

No matter what it is you want to accomplish in life, if it's something bigger than your existence, the work will involve others. The strength of your collaboration and the ultimate outcome of the work you accomplish together is inextricably linked to how you see them—no matter how they see you. Ultimately, leadership is less about imparting something great to others and more about extracting something great from them, something that already exists within them though they can't yet see it. But you can. Here's where that journey began for me . . .

CHAPTER 1

TWO KINDS OF GROWTH

"Take her home and treat her like everybody else."

The doctor's advice to my parents, given on the cold winter morning I was born, helped set the course of my life. The doctor could see I had clubfoot, but X-rays showed I had something else, a form of dwarfism called *achondroplasia*, usually referred to as simply "achon" (pronounced a-kon). This was the 1960s, so my parents had no frame of reference for what the diagnosis meant. If we're being honest, neither did the doctors. Even though achon is the most common of the approximately two hundred types of dwarfism, this was over five decades ago, when you didn't see a lot of little people in public. There's no doubt in my mind the doctor was out of his element when faced with my condition, which made his recommendation all the more remarkable.

His perspective gave my parents hope and direction, although I tend to think they would have taken that route regardless. They seemed built to handle pretty much anything. Even though both were in their early twenties when I was born, there wasn't much they hadn't already seen and conquered. Seemingly unfazed, they took me home and dedicated their lives to doing what the doctor had prescribed—so successfully that, for years, I never knew I was different from anyone else.

Halloween was my first clue. We lived in a middle-class neighborhood of about forty houses in East Peoria, Illinois. My younger sister, older brother, and I slipped into character each year, and away we'd go, trick-or-treating with our parents leading the way. I was out-of-my-mind excited every year, but by about four years old, a subtle question had arisen in my mind: How come every neighbor knew it was me behind the ghost costume? I mean, my face was hidden . . . and yet every time a door opened, it was, "Hi, Michele! Come on in!"

I also wondered why my trick-or-treating stint was so curiously short compared to my siblings' epic trek. Three houses and I was done. My legs couldn't go any farther. In contrast, my brother and sister hiked to every house in the neighborhood. Our parents supplemented my candy spoils to make it fair, so I never complained. But I didn't understand why.

Then I went to kindergarten.

I leapt out of the car when we arrived at Robein Grade School for my first day of school. As my mom and I walked down two long hallways and the classroom came into view, I straightened my shoulders and stuck out my chest like I owned the place. If you've seen the BBC clip of the professor being interviewed when his young daughter comes strutting into his office in the background, you know about how I looked. I shoved open my classroom door and announced, "Hello!" in a shrill voice. The teacher grinned as she greeted me. Then she directed me to the other kids, who were playing in a circle, while she talked to my mom. I scurried over and plopped down next to them.

"Hey!" I bubbled. I couldn't believe my luck. Contrary to some kids who enter their first classroom terrified, I'd been awaiting this day my entire life. And I'd finally made it. I got right down to the business of playing with my new friends.

More kids arrived and filled the classroom, and we bustled about while our teacher greeted the parents. I was chatting up everyone who'd listen when a blond boy in blue shorts and a white shirt stopped next to me.

"Why are you so little?" he asked. "You look funny."

I kept chatting away. I didn't think he was talking to me.

He said it louder and craned over me to show that he was bigger.

"What are you talking about?" I said. "I'm not little."

"Yeah, why do you look funny?" the girl on my other side echoed. "What's the matter with you?"

I just stood there.

To break the sudden silence, I went back to playing. It was too late. Now every kid in the circle had stopped playing and was staring at me. I can still feel the moment in my bones. I glanced over my outfit, thinking maybe it was my clothes.

I still didn't speak, but the air had changed. The other kids busied themselves, still glancing over their shoulders to try and understand. My face and shoulders fell. My stomach churned. I looked around for someone else to play with, and that's when I realized a new circle had formed, and I was standing outside it.

In that instant I morphed from a confident young girl into a scared, self-conscious one. Isn't it profound what a single event can do to a person? Confusion enveloped me throughout the rest of that day, like a fog that wouldn't lift. For the first couple of hours, I tried to rise above it. I'd raise my hand with an answer to the teacher's question. Then I'd speak and notice the head tilts and stares from the desks beside me. By 10:00 a.m. naptime, I was a bystander. I laid my head on the small square of brown carpet and didn't close my eyes. I could only replay the phrases I'd heard and the looks I'd seen, over and over in my head. Eventually, the weight of fear and uncertainty was too much for me. After naptime was over, I kept my hands folded on my desk and my mouth shut.

Isn't it profound what a single event can do to a person?

I beelined for my mom's car as soon as the teacher dismissed us that afternoon. I crawled in the front seat, sat up, and looked straight ahead.

"How did it go?" my mom asked as she put the car in drive.

"Is there something wrong with me?" I countered. "What does 'retarded' mean?"

She paused in a way she had never paused before that day. It was probably only seconds, but it may as well have been three hours. Her silence frightened me. I know now that she wanted to say the right thing. And that she had been thinking about her answer for five years.

"Well," she finally began, "you *are* smaller than everybody else, Michele—it's how God made you."

She said it so matter-of-factly, in the same way she told me, "It'll only be a little sting," when I had to get a shot. Her tone took me aback.

"But you can still do anything and everything," she continued. "Keep getting to know people, and if they get to know you, they won't think of you as being different."

We came to a stoplight and she turned toward me and looked right into my eyes, as if doing so would maximize my comprehension of what she said next. "Because the truth is, we all have our differences, honey. Some are just more obvious than others."

I would discover that my mom was right. But not before discovering that being different wasn't as easy as it sounded. Recognizing your differences isn't as difficult as embracing them, let alone learning that they can be your greatest advantage.

That first day of kindergarten drew a big, fat line in the sand. Once I crossed it, there was no going back. The news that I was, and would remain, smaller than others my entire life was both confusing and shocking to my young heart, and it instantly darkened the world outside my home. The realization marked the beginning of a new journey from acceptance to confidence to understanding that looking up to others is much more than a matter of physical stature.

The journey would take me a while. It had begun on that first day of school, but the majority of my early progress occurred at our kitchen table.

Every night while I was growing up, my family gathered

in the modest, linoleum-floored kitchen at 6:00 p.m. There we took our seats around the oval oak table and ate together. Over the adventurous concoctions my mom whipped up, we'd take turns sharing about our day. My mom was always curious and always reading, and she would usually share a nugget of wisdom she'd learned. My dad would tell us tales from the factory floor at Caterpillar (CAT), where he worked as a forklift operator and, later, as a foreman. My older brother, younger sister, and I would spill the latest school gossip—for me especially, something notable always seemed to happen—and my mom and dad were genuinely interested in what we were experiencing. (Remember when you were young and the most exciting days at school were when somebody puked?) Of course, they also asked what *else* we'd learned in class. Who did we hang out with at recess? How did we feel? What were we struggling with? It became something I counted on, this allotted time and place to let down any walls I'd built up to protect myself during the day. It was a safe place, a sanctuary of sorts, filled with people who knew the difference between hearing and listening. Even we kids came to understand this difference.

Dinner at the kitchen table was also an important ritual because it's where I began to fully comprehend the breadth of my family members' lives. I was no longer just seeing them in passing. I was getting to know them, really know who they were, how they thought and hurt and dreamed. Though I sensed from a distance the emotional, physical, and financial tax that my circumstances had on them, at dinner I got to see the full spectrum of their colored lives. And they got to see mine. In that way, those precious hours around the table were as life-giving as they were lifesaving, especially as the doctor visits increased. I came to see that, despite being constantly in need of medical attention, life was not all about me.

We had my mom to thank for the nightly tradition. Growing up, she and her family had relocated constantly. Her dad, a lanky, thick-haired Swede, toggled between seasonal work as a carpenter and intermittent entrepreneurship throughout her childhood, owning a single tavern at three different times in Minnesota, and holding various other jobs in North and South Dakota. Having grown up the son of first-generation immigrants during the Great Depression, he'd learned to take no opportunity lightly, and he moved the family as often as was necessary to ensure income. One of the only consistencies during my mom's early years was sitting around the kitchen table for family dinner. In a postwar, mid-century America that seemed to be changing more rapidly than anyone could predict, it was formative to always have the stability of an evening meal together. But—such was her life—even that changed.

When she was fourteen, my mom's parents sent her alone on a twenty-four-hour bus ride from their small town in the prairieland of Minnesota to Peoria, Illinois, where her older sister and brother-in-law were about to have their second baby. Her sister was going to need help caring for the first child while she tended to her newborn, and apparently my middle school–age mom was the answer.

Maybe it wasn't as crazy as it sounds to me. My mom was used to being resourceful. The frequent relocation during her childhood may have forced it on her, but she hadn't shrunk from the uncertainty. It seemed to strengthen her. The harsh Midwestern winters made her resilient. The odd jobs made her capable. All of this prepared her for a near and distant future. In the end, she navigated the solo trip to Peoria like a champ, which included changing bus stations in Chicago after she'd been told she wouldn't have to, and then having no money for a taxi when there was no one to pick her up at her destination. Her sister had no phone, so my mom sat in a cotton dress and stockings and waited at the outdoor bus station, which was no more than a metal awning and a wooden bench. One hour later, her brother, who also lived in the area, showed up. When my mom finally stepped foot in her older sister's home well into the evening, she offered no complaints and jumped right into a maternal responsibility that didn't typically befall a teenager. She'd been born with more moxie than most girls her age. And she continued to grow.

Years later, after meeting and marrying my father, the same sister and husband fell ill with tuberculosis. They were quarantined individually and apart from their four children. In order for the kids to not be placed in foster care, my parents took them in. In her midtwenties, my mom was caring for five kids under age seven.

Long after my aunt and uncle recovered and my cousins moved back into their home, our fridge still featured a picture of my young mom with five towheaded children gathered in front of her. Her hair is already stark white—courtesy, I'm sure, of the weight of responsibility and various near disasters, like once discovering my three-year-old brother standing in the middle of the interstate that ran right outside their front door. Next to the photo was an index card with my mom's handwriting: "Start where you are. Use what you have. Do what you can."

That became a mantra of mine as I navigated adolescence. It was either that or accept a limited life at home, with siblings for friends and parents for teachers. This would have been the more common choice. In the late 1960s and early 1970s, the only little people in the public eye were on a television set or at a circus. My mom wouldn't allow me to hide, though I often tried, and she saw much more for my life than the average American did. With her direct but loving encouragement, I settled into a routine at school and there was a sense of normalcy to my days. My comparative differences were still, increasingly, prevalent. My legs weren't long enough to walk up the steps of the school bus, so I crawled up on my hands and knees, like a toddler climbing stairs. I also had to keep to the outskirts of the school hallways so kids wouldn't accidentally plow into me, which happened from time to time, once knocking me out cold. Eventually, everyone got used to seeing me, and I wasn't worthy of their whispers and stares anymore. Within the safe confines of school, I was the short girl. So what? Been there, seen that.

"Start where you are. Use what you have. Do what you can."

And then it got even better.

One day during second grade, the teacher introduced my class to a game called Around the World. It was a math game that used flash cards, and the teacher would divide us into pairs and show us some type of math problem. Each duo competed once, and whoever answered first out of the two got to move on in the competition. Like math's version of college basketball's March Madness, the competitive pool halved and halved again until eventually there was only one person remaining.

The incentive to win, aside from pride, was that your animal got to come out of the cage. All the kids had cut out animals from a magazine and pinned them to a plain bulletin board that served as the "cage." If you won the game, your animal got to be pinned on the grassy area (green construction paper) of the bulletin board, outside the cage, until the following week. What freedom!

What do you know? It turned out that math was my forte. My animal was nearly always the last one standing. I'd get all the problems right, ahead of each competitor, and win the game. This meant my animal—I'd of course chosen a giraffe—was a permanent fixture on the lush green construction paper. There wasn't much that compared to the pride I felt in seeing my lanky representative get pinned in position on the green paper outside the cage. Except, of course, my pride about being good at math.

I had a distinct knack for numbers, and it led to the most significant development at that point in my young life: my schoolmates' description of me changed. No longer was the common refrain, "Michele is small." It became, "Michele is smart." It was the first time in school that I was defined by something other than my height, the first time I was seen as something besides a little person, and it confirmed that what my parents had told me was true: I am more than my size. This meant that—aside from perhaps a WNBA star or a runway model—I could be anything.

It would take me a little longer to understand that others didn't always agree with this assessment. It would also take some time to wholly believe it myself.

◦　◦　◦

One summer afternoon, my siblings and I spent the day at my grandma's house. It was a hot day that called for an ice cream cone, so we walked to the nearby ice cream shop after lunch. As we walked back home, we passed two middle school boys in a parking lot. I was focused on my delicious cone and didn't notice them gawking. Then one of them swung around and shoved me from behind, so hard it knocked me off my feet. In a flash my face was flat on the asphalt and my ice cream was upside down and melting. My brother and sister started crying. When I pushed up on my elbows and looked back, the boys were laughing.

"Take that, midget!" one cackled.

My grandma gathered herself and helped me up.

"Come on," she said as she brushed me off. "We've just got to go. Come on."

As we hurried off, I started sobbing and the boys began chanting, "Midget! Midget! Midget!" I'd never heard the word before that day.

It was the first time I'd ever been intentionally targeted. I'd been called names before and been knocked down more than a few times, but no one had ever attacked me on purpose. It was malicious and confusing. I felt demoralized, and the experience shook me to my core.

That night at dinner, my siblings and I recounted the story to my parents. I saw my mom's shoulders drop slightly, but when she saw I was looking at her, they lifted back up.

"People make fun of things they don't understand," she said, reaching over and squeezing my hand. "I know it might be hard to realize this right now, but you're a far bigger person than those boys today."

What happened that afternoon stayed with me long after the handprint on my back faded. All these years later, I can see that their cruel treatment of me stemmed from fear and ignorance. They couldn't fit what they'd seen into a box they understood, so they made a presumption about my worth. But

Comfort is the wrong choice when it comes to how we see others.

the way they chose to react was a sheer reflection of their own insecurity. Why would they look up to me when looking down on me felt more comfortable? I understand the choice from a human-nature standpoint; we're drawn to comfort. But comfort is the wrong choice when it comes to how we see others.

.   .   .

Having gray hair, bearing one skin tone or another, wearing a suit, being shy, visible tattoos—these all create an instant profile in the minds of others. Yet it doesn't tell half the story of who you are or what you're capable of. That's how life is. As we look at the people around us, we label them in order to understand our environment as quickly as possible. However, we begin to grow when we learn to see beyond the labels.

I'm a woman who wears size 1 shoes. I'm as tall as a second grader. I roll around in a motorized scooter or, if I'm feeling frisky, I use crutches. The vertebrae in my neck are fused due to a death-defying fall I'll tell you about later. This means my head doesn't turn unless my entire upper body does, which is a little freaky or funny or both. Can you imagine what labels the sight of me conjures up when I come rolling into a boardroom or clicking down an office corridor? I've seen them all in the faces of others over a lifetime—from the head tilts of my kindergarten classmates to the chin tucks of uncertainty to the bulging eyes of those who look like they've seen a zombie. Some reactions make me giggle. I've learned they're not personal; they're the result of an incomplete perspective. That's why I always try to take initiative to broaden another's perspective. "Hi," I say with a smile and an outstretched hand. "I'm Michele." The other person's eyes usually soften, and their perspective expands as we squeeze each other's palm. If we stay on this path, mystery turns to adventure. Our minds and hearts begin to open. Bigger things can happen. They certainly have for me.

Four decades after discovering that I had a mind for numbers, I found myself in the Oval Office for a meeting with President Obama. The business world was built for attractive, sprightly five- and six-foot-somethings who can walk with ease and authority. No one expects to see size 1s and a motorized scooter, but there I was, with a dozen other qualified people, discussing an education task force with the president of the United States. It was a "pinch me" moment.

As I looked around at the broad range of diversity in the room—we were young and old; black, brown, and white; women and men; tall and short—I thought back to my first day of kindergarten and how my mom's advice during the car ride home may have been the most important she ever gave me. "Get to know them," she'd said. I eventually realized why this advice was repeated so often. Everyone already had a perception of me before I met them. I was little. My voice was squeaky. I was different. In the eyes of many, I was too little, too squeaky, and too different to accomplish big things. But now I was rolling my short, squeaking self to the head of a table where the most powerful man in the free world also sat.

How had I gotten from that first difficult day of kindergarten to there?

Constant growth. Which is irony in its purest form.

By the time I was ten, I was physically done growing. That was it. I was four feet tall and finished. I remember going to my annual orthopedic appointment, eager to see that I'd grown another inch since the last visit. That was the usual benchmark—one inch a year, give or take. At each appointment I looked forward to saying, "See, Mommy? I'm not going to be little. I got my inch!" I had secretly held out hope that my being smaller was all a big misunderstanding.

Then, at my ten-year-old checkup, I hadn't grown any taller. Not even a centimeter. The doctor confirmed my fate in his booming voice.

"Well, Michele, it looks like you've gone as far as you can go."

I didn't believe him. Back then I was saucy when I didn't get what I wanted (okay, still am). I made him measure again. Same thing. No more inches. I was devastated. I was going to live my life as a little person after all. While all of my peers would eventually transform into average-size adults, I would be stuck looking like a second grader. I left the doctor's office with one persistent question in my head. As I looked out the window on the car ride home, I blurted it out. "Now what?" I asked my mom.

"What do you mean?" she said.

"I'm done growing. Now what do I do?"

"Michele," she said with a perfect blend of compassion and strength, "that's just your size. It's not who you are. You can continue to grow as much as you choose to."

Somehow, I knew what she was saying, even at ten. It washed over me like a sudden summer breeze. I immediately grasped that while I couldn't control the limits of my physical growth, I could still choose to grow in other ways.

Growth is never just physical, is it? In fact, most of us are done growing physically right when we become adults. Isn't that an interesting twist in life? We're done growing upward in the first quarter of life, but growth is still necessary if we want the last three-quarters of our lives to make an impact, if we want to discover and accomplish the things we're created to do, if we want to meet the high mark of our full potential. Maybe physical growth stops as adulthood starts to remind us that the growth that ultimately matters isn't on the outside.

There are two kinds of growth: we grow up on the outside and we grow up on the inside. After about twenty years old, the only growth we can control is the inside, though some continue tinkering with the outside for years. Which one matters most to you?

In an ironic twist, I was the largest newborn of the three children in my family. But eventually my brother and sister passed me on our doctor's growth charts. It's always interesting to hear parents

Maybe physical growth stops as adulthood starts to remind us that the growth that ultimately matters isn't on the outside.

discuss where their kids fall on those charts. While there's no imminent health concern if a child measures in the twentieth percentile in height, many parents seem disappointed and even dejected with this news. On the other hand, learning your child is in the ninetieth percentile seems bragworthy. It's cause for celebration, like, "My child is headed for big things!" I think we all understand the inclination parents have to hope their children are tall—height does provide an advantage in the world. But it's only an opening advantage. Ultimately, if you're stunted on the inside, it won't matter if you're six-foot-anything.

I had a distinct advantage in having to come to terms with this perspective very early in life. Once physical growth was no longer an option, I had a choice to make: Would I lament my percentile on the chart, or would I find other ways to grow? Although I had to search out my answer when I was only ten, the same question is posed to everyone throughout life. How do you prioritize your growth? Are you focused on the outside or on the inside? Your answer is a good indication of how you assign value to others. We all tend to celebrate in others what we value most in ourselves.

CHAPTER 2

THERE IS NO SUCH THING AS KNOWLEDGE AT FIRST SIGHT

We use the phrase "love at first sight" often, but when I see the audacious way some people treat each other these days, I wonder whether more might believe in knowledge at first sight. How much can we know about a person from one photo, one post, or one passing glance? We like to say "a picture is worth a thousand words," but if that's true, then a person ought to be worth a thousand pictures. Knowing anyone takes more than one sighting. I realize this is easier said than done.

Sometimes being a little person feels like being famous,

except nobody knows your name. You garner stares, most of which aren't remotely subtle, and then people sit and watch you. They might look away for a time, but their eyes eventually return. Are they intrigued? Disgusted? Impressed? Sometimes I glance over at someone who's particularly glued to me and give a quick wave with my little hand. The priceless reaction, from embarrassment to sheer terror, is my entertainment. Forgive me, Father. Maybe I shouldn't do it, but a little private levity goes a long way.

While famous people often get approached for a photo, an autograph, or a proclamation of love, being a little person doesn't evoke the same response. I don't usually know where I stand when it comes to public opinion. Do you ever feel this way? It's not like people are interrupting me during a dinner out because they want to shake my hand and express their admiration for my work.

Don't break out the violin. I'm not complaining, merely observing. I'm plenty used to the reaction that my presence can conjure up. I understand it too. Believe it or not, I reacted the same way when I came face-to-face with a little person for the first time.

At one of our extended family gatherings in mid-1978 (I was twelve), my cousin told my mom and me that a student at her high school, named Gary, was a little person. My mom's reaction—"Really!"—revealed that while she'd known there were other little people in the world, she hadn't found any to show me. Throughout grade school, I'd repeatedly asked my parents if I was the only little person in the world. Though they assured me there were others—my doctor went as far as to say there were "lots more"—I had no proof. I had never seen another person like me. I couldn't browse the internet or tune in to *Little People, Big World*. Tattoo (played by a little person named Hervé Villechaize) wasn't yet proclaiming, "Da plane! Da plane!" on the TV show *Fantasy Island*, which would premiere its first season a few months later. In a roundabout way, the existence of this mysterious other little person validated something inside me. My mom turned to me and asked if I wanted to meet Gary.

"Yes!" I said without hesitation. Right then and there, my mom made a plan with my cousin to get in touch with Gary's parents, who, it turned out, lived only a ten-minute drive from us.

Three weeks later, my parents and I pulled up to the curb at Gary's house. With my face pressed eagerly against the window, excitement suddenly knotted in my throat the second my dad turned off the engine. For years, I'd been told I wasn't the only one, and now, on the verge of confirming it was true, I suddenly wasn't sure if I wanted to puke, celebrate, or run away. I clammed up and followed my parents to the front door.

The meeting became more vivid in the years after it happened, but at the time, it felt like an out-of-body experience. I wasn't my usual outgoing self with Gary or his parents. I gave a wave and a quick hello and then retreated into my shell like a turtle. I'm sure it had something to do with the typical middle school girl shyness that can manifest in the presence of a high school boy. It was more than that though.

When we sat down in our own kitchen for dinner that night, I still hadn't said much about meeting Gary, and I wasn't sure if I would. As my siblings debriefed their days, I nodded like I was listening, but I was in my own head. The truth is, I was still unsure of my feelings and didn't know what to say. My mom must have known, because when it came time for me to talk about my day, she reached for a copy of the *Reader's Digest* sitting nearby and summarized an article she'd read weeks before about an organization called Little People of America, or LPA. Gary's parents had mentioned the organization earlier that day. My mom explained that she'd written the LPA to get some more information about it and received a letter in the mail that very morning. She pulled a white envelope from between the *Reader's Digest* pages and slid her chair next to mine, and we opened the letter together.

We learned the LPA was a support system and resource center for little people and their families. There were locally based chapters throughout the United States, and Peoria was in the Little Prairie chapter. Periodic chapter meetings were held in Springfield, only an hour south of where we lived, at the house of a woman named JoAnne.

My brain quickly computed what this meant. Not only did other little people actually exist but there were enough of us to form an organization. And a car ride could take me to them. My mom showed me on the letter where it listed some upcoming meeting dates, and we made a plan right then and there to attend one in a couple weeks' time.

On the drive to Springfield, a mix of hope and angst battled inside me. Meeting Gary had been something of a novelty, what I imagine it feels like to finally spot a grizzly bear in the wild or a great white on a dive in the Pacific. I had been wondering about seeing a "Gary" my entire life, and then it finally happened. The thought of meeting a group of people like me was something entirely different. It meant something else that I couldn't quite identify yet.

The hour-long drive passed in minutes, and before I knew it, we were parking in front of a two-story, brick-and-siding house with a white garage and a red front door. I've never been a swift walker, but the walk from our car to that red door felt like slow motion. My heart bumped against my chest. I already knew I wasn't the only one anymore. But somehow—maybe because Gary was only a couple of years older than me—the implications hadn't fully set in. I tried to take a deep breath and found it difficult. I honestly couldn't tell if this was the same reaction I always had when walking into the company of people who'd never seen me, or something else. As we approached, my dad reached his thick, calloused hand back to me, and when he felt my hand in his, he enveloped it gently and firmly.

We came to the door, and my dad knocked three times. Seconds later I could hear footsteps heading our way. Heat rose from my shoulders to my head.

JoAnne opened the door with a big smile. She was an attractive woman in her fifties with light brown hair and a certain grace that put me at ease for a brief moment. My senses were still on overdrive, though, and I could tell by this time that my body was numbing itself for protection. I wanted to run but instead I squeezed my dad's hand tighter. JoAnne led us from the entryway into her living room, where about a dozen little people of all ages, and their families, stood around socializing. I froze. My legs were cemented to the ground, and my mind went blank. I remember my eyes locking onto a young man in his late teens standing by the couch. He was behind his mother's legs, peering at the floor. He was smaller than me. I stared and I knew I was staring, but I couldn't stop myself. This might sound strange but, for the first time, I could see what I actually looked like in the world.

I was stunned.

We really are *different*, I thought. *I get why people stare.*

It wasn't just that we were short. We looked . . . different.

Why this light bulb hadn't popped on when I met Gary, I'll never know; but now, standing in a room full of people like me, who were standing next to parents and siblings of typical size, I suddenly knew why I drew so much attention in public.

My parents did all the talking for the next two hours. I offered up no more than a few obligatory hellos. It was rare for me not to have a lot to say (something that remains true to this day), but the setting felt too overwhelming. Too much to soak in. My worldview had been forever changed, but I wasn't yet mature enough to comprehend what it might mean.

My silence continued on the ride home. And into the next day, and the next. I was full of inner dialogue, wrestling over whether or not I wanted to be involved in LPA. Here's what it came down to, although it existed on a more subconscious level than I could articulate at the time: If I became part of that community, it meant I'd have to accept who I was. It meant I'd officially be a little person. But more than that, I'd officially, and in no uncertain terms, be different. And not subtly different. Quite obviously different. I wasn't so sure about embracing that. Could I handle standing out in the most ironic sort of way?

As the days and weeks went on, there was a nagging thought that kept making its way back to me: When I was around the people from LPA, I wasn't different. For those couple of hours, surrounded by a dozen others like me, it was almost as if we were the "normal" ones and it was everyone else who stood out. Whether I wanted to admit it or not, while the experience was emotionally complicated, it had also been a respite because I learned I wasn't alone in my differences.

I made the decision to go back to LPA, and it remains one of the best decisions I've ever made. Even though I had the love and support from my family, and even though I didn't often dwell in a place of feeling "less than," there was something about having a community of people who inherently understood me. Who understood exactly what I was going through. We saw eye to eye—literally and figuratively—and that kinship set the stage for something I'd spend years pondering, and even more years trying to answer: How much better would the world be if we all weren't just looked at, but were actually seen the same way those who understand us are? There's a profound leap we can all make when we finally understand that there's no such thing as knowledge at first sight.

It's perfectly normal—wise, even—to be part of a close cohort with whom you don't stand out. The goal, however, should never be to form your sole existence in a bubble. The goal should always be to expand from close cohort to diverse community. Investing only in people exactly like you will ensure that your growth slows and eventually hits a ceiling as familiarity and comfort reign. That doesn't mean you can't learn from people who have something in common with you. It just means that you won't learn as much from them as you will from people who are different from you.

It's natural and more comfortable to be with friends and family who require little effort. We need environments that are safe and stable if for no other reason than to rest our emotions and recharge our spirits. We can also, however, become overly attached to comfortable crowds. When that happens, it's all too easy to swell with self-absorption and arrogance. Left unchecked, we'll eventually focus on our kind alone, and we'll lose sight of the others outside our microcosm—we may even come to resent the outsiders and the intrusion to life that they represent. This precarious existence was captured well when, in 1957, Dr. Martin Luther King Jr. told the congregation at Dexter Avenue Baptist Church, "An individual has not begun to live until he can rise above the narrow horizons of his particular individualistic concerns to the broader concerns of all humanity. And this is one of the big problems of life, that so many people never quite get to the point of rising above self."[1]

Rising above ourselves begins with a broader perspective, not on our own desires and dreams, but on those of others. When we zoom out from our own existence and then zoom in on the lives of others, we quickly discover that people unlike

How much better would the world be if we weren't just looked at, but were actually seen the same way those who understand us are?

us can increase our breadth of knowledge and depth of experience. People different from us offer new perspectives, new ideas, new sources of growth. Those unlike us open our eyes to greater possibilities; they can even forge a path to our own healing.

CHAPTER 3

SEEING OTHERS
TAKES SACRIFICE

There's a critical difference between having sight and seeing something for what it is. Every day, we scan our environments for sights we can explain, objects and activities we understand well. As we age from children into adults, the scope of what we can understand grows exponentially. Eventually, we learn to see our way through life pretty naturally. Most of what we see we recognize right away—cars, the bank, stoplights, trees, and various animals. The trouble is, we tend to apply this instant recognition to people. Our sight fails us when we don't learn to look further into the faces and figures we see around us.

When my parents and I met Gary for the first time, it was late summer, and he'd recently returned from Johns Hopkins after having his leg casts removed. He'd had leg surgery in

June, performed by an orthopedic surgeon named Dr. Kopits. Gary's family had found Dr. Kopits through the LPA, and when his name came up, they strongly recommended that my parents contact him.

Gary's family couldn't have known how perfect the timing of their recommendation was. My family had already spent the previous two months in five different doctors' offices at places such as Mayo Clinic and Shriners Hospital, seeking recommendations for treating my hip dysplasia, which had become more problematic since I'd stopped growing. When we returned home from Gary's, my mom called Dr. Kopits's office for an appointment.

Dr. Kopits was a unique physician in the medical world for his vision to enable people with dwarfism to thrive. Born in Budapest, Hungary, where his father and grandfather had been orthopedic surgeons before him, he moved to Buenos Aires in 1960 to study medicine at the Universidad de Buenos Aires. In 1964, the year before I was born, he moved to Baltimore for his internship at Union Memorial and then residency at Johns Hopkins, where he remained for two decades. While at Johns Hopkins, Dr. Kopits encountered patients seeking genetic counseling, in particular children who suffered from dwarfism.[1]

Few if any advances had been made in the treatment of dwarfism in the twelve years since I'd been born. There was no known specialist, at least that we could find—only well-trained physicians who still treated the physical challenges little people faced in the same manner they treated a patient without dwarfism. Where other doctors shied away from the many unknowns my condition presented, Dr. Kopits saw a profound opportunity.

By 1975, three years before we met him, more than 80 percent of his patients were little people, and he had developed new surgical instruments and techniques for straightening misaligned hips, knees, ankles, and spines.[2] His patients came not just from every part of the country to see him but from every part of the world.

We had to wait over a month for our appointment, an understandable consequence of his dedication. When we entered his office that September, I was filled with wonder. Everything there was made for little people. The chairs were lower; the shelves with magazines and toys were accessible; the exam tables could be reached with a simple step stool; the water fountain was chest level. Once we took a seat in his office, he immediately pulled up an empty chair in front of me and asked about school. For twenty minutes, we discussed what I was studying, what I enjoyed (math, of course), and what I wanted to do when I grew up. The experience was night-and-day different from the previous doctors' visits that year.

Dr. Kopits once told the *Washington Post*, "The preached doctrine is that you cannot be a good physician if you get emotionally involved with your patients. My doctrine is that you cannot be a good physician unless you do get emotionally involved."[3] To say he was a talented doctor wouldn't do him justice. There were many talented doctors during that time. He was an innovator and a godsend. But most accurately, he was an extraordinary man in an influential position who saw me for both my distinctions and my common human condition. To Dr. Kopits, I wasn't a patient suffering with dwarfism; I was a middle school girl trying to understand herself and her place in the world, who had a physical challenge that didn't have to stand in the way. For the first time I wasn't a problem to solve; I was potential to unleash. I could see a bigger picture of my life in Dr. Kopits's bright, confident eyes. The way he saw me forged a new perspective in my young mind: my dwarfism wasn't the real challenge—my perspective was. Through him, the scope of my future broadened into the realm of "a normal life." That might sound weird, but before meeting Dr. Kopits, I wasn't thinking about what I wanted to be when I grew up. I wasn't thinking about having a career and a house and all that came with becoming an adult one day. I was trying to figure out how to not get pointed at or knocked down in my school's hallways. Despite my parents' constant encouragement, I was still on the defense, and I felt my biggest goal in life was to become the best defender I could. In Dr. Kopits's eyes, I could see that I'd been shortsighted.

At the end of our conversation, he explained that he'd need me to sit through a series of X-rays and tests to understand the best course of treatment for my hips. I was expecting maybe an hour on a couple of cold, metal tables, holding my breath in various positions, like my previous experiences. The tests Dr. Kopits ordered—twelve in all—took two days.

On the third day, we gathered in a huge conference room: me, my parents, Dr. Kopits, and his nurse practitioner. My X-rays were arranged in rows on two backlit walls. Dr. Kopits walked us through what my issues were as he pointed at specific pictures. He explained that the type of dwarfism I had was not achondroplasia, as I'd been told. He admitted he wasn't sure what form I had but that it was a rarer form having the characteristics of multiple types of dwarfism. (Two years later, he determined I had what's called *metatropic dysplasia*, a rare form with only one hundred known cases in history, which has led to me calling myself "Heinz 57" among my little friends, because of this odd mixture.) He then said he believed he could help me. It took nearly two hours for him to walk us through everything and answer all of our questions.

There's a spectrum of challenges for little people, ranging from extremely debilitating ones to no issues at all. Results also showed that I was somewhere in the middle and suffered primarily from severe hip dysplasia, which basically means that my hip socket and the ball at the end of my upper thigh bone aren't close enough together to keep my hips from dislocating. Dr. Kopits recommended osteotomies—effectively, surgical dislocation, reconstruction, and relocation—on my hips first, then, after about six weeks, a similar surgery on both knees. If all went well, he said, it was possible but not certain that we wouldn't have to operate on my ankles.

Upon hearing Dr. Kopits detail the seemingly endless string of surgeries, the atmosphere in his office changed from hopeful to overwhelming. I was consumed with one thought: *How am I going to attend school and make it to eighth-grade graduation?* A bit more was going through my parents' minds.

They took everything in, then stood up and thanked Dr. Kopits for his time. Over handshakes, they promised to think about all he had said. What made their reaction so equivocal was that Dr. Kopits's advice was a big departure from the other advice we'd received—from physical therapy to "wait and see" how I felt as I aged. In hindsight, I now know the other doctors didn't know what to do with me. I was out of their element and outside the scope of their protocol. In the context of traditional medicine, that was certainly true of

Dr. Kopits at one point in his career. But he looked outside that context and sought to learn something he didn't already know. One of the most common hurdles to seeing others in a positive light is an unwillingness to look past what is easy to see. When our eyes are all we use to see other people, we aren't looking with every resource we have.

When our eyes are all we use to see other people, we aren't looking with every resource we have.

We drove back to our Baltimore hotel in silence that afternoon. I think we were all in shock that of all the doctors we'd seen, the one who seemed the most capable had recommended the most complex course of action. My mom headed up to our room, and my dad and I walked to the lobby to get a drink. My face was red and my brows furrowed; I could not get my head around how all the surgeries were going to happen without me missing my last year of middle school. I wanted to attend high school like everyone else. My dad got us a table in the modest hotel restaurant, and there he let me vent. I toggled between, "Why do I have to do this?" and "This just isn't going to work, Daddy," offering up school as my most compelling piece of evidence. He sat calmly with his hands folded on the table, nodding occasionally and never breaking eye contact. He didn't try to talk me out of anything. He also didn't concede.

When we returned to the room thirty minutes later, my emotions were in check until I couldn't find my mom. I peeked in the bathroom, but she wasn't there. It wasn't a big room, so I worried about where she'd gone. Then I remembered the small balcony. I walked over and pulled the curtains open, and there she was. Her arms were cradling her midsection like she was in pain. As soon as I began sliding the glass door, she shot up from her chair and glanced over at me. Her eyes were bloodshot. She'd been crying. The only time I'd seen my mom cry was when her father passed away. I was so taken aback by the sight of her wet eyes and splotchy face that I immediately started bawling. She reached out her arm and pulled me in tight.

"I don't—I don't understand—why—I need—all the—surrrrgery," I heaved in staccato.

"I know, honey," she replied softly, stroking my hair. "It's all difficult to understand, but we need to do all we can for your health."

Suddenly a thought hit me: this wasn't just hard for me; it might actually be harder on my parents. They were going to have to deal with the stress of missing work and the financial burden of these tests and surgeries, not to mention still parenting my two siblings while they were giving so much attention to me. There was also the pain of seeing me, their middle child, whom they loved unconditionally, struggling with a medical condition few seemed to understand.

After much discussion over the next two days, my parents helped me see that what Dr. Kopits had recommended could improve my quality of life if it worked. None of us knew then how true that was, or to what degree our intersection with him would alter my existence forever.

· · ·

We waited nine months, until after my eighth-grade graduation in June, and then drove back to Johns Hopkins and Dr. Kopits for my first of many surgeries. I was geared up for hell. We'd been told each hip would require approximately ten hours under the knife. I imagine technology has come a long way since, but back then the way it worked was that you went in to get the first hip fixed and then spent seven days in a cast from your toes to your chest. Then you went back under the knife and had the second hip done. Then it was back in the body cast for several more weeks. Even thinking about it now makes me want to throw my size 1s at the wall. All I could think about back then was how my classmates would be lounging by the pool or on family vacation at some glorious beach. Meanwhile, I'd be mummified and envisioning shapes in the popcorn ceiling all summer.

My parents hadn't filled me in on the details. I knew I needed at least four surgeries, but I thought that meant over time. I prepared myself to get through one surgery that summer and that was that. Done for the year. Not so. Seven days after my first surgery, my mom spilled the beans that I was now going to have the second hip done. "*What?*" I exclaimed shrilly, as only a thirteen-year-old can. "You've got to be kidding! This is torture!"

The good news—a small victory by comparison—was that after my merciless second hip surgery, the doctors allowed me to return home and spend the rest of my fossilized summer in my own bed. There was only one problem. My parents didn't know how they'd get me back to Peoria. The family Buick wasn't a suitable vehicle for a petrified little person who couldn't be jostled. I couldn't fly commercially because I had to lie flat. There was also the unfortunate cartwheel position that the cast put me in, which wasn't doing wonders for my self-esteem.

My dad had been working at Caterpillar for nearly fifteen years by this time, and he was well respected among his colleagues. He shared with his boss the looming predicament of transporting his daughter home from Baltimore, and then asked if there was a way the company could help. His boss worked up the ladder. Three days later, he came back to my dad, offering the use of a company jet.

My first plane ride would be on a Cessna Citation I, a twin-engine aircraft that was a heck of a lot faster than a car. Maintenance removed all of the seats down the left side of the cabin and installed a hospital bed in their place. Five days after my second surgery, the plane landed in Baltimore with my dad and a company nurse on board. Meanwhile, my mom had arranged for an ambulance to take us from the hospital to meet the plane.

All went perfectly until my dad and two EMTs carried me up the steps to board. I was giggling and said, "Hey Daddy, isn't this great? I'm getting swept off my feet!" He laughed with me until we reached the door and realized that in my spread-eagle position, my legs didn't fit through the opening.

I could see the worried looks on the men's faces as they backed my upper body out of the door. All these moving parts had been orchestrated to transport me home, some with real financial costs, and now they couldn't get the patient onto the plane. With me still lying in their arms, the three stood there, staring at the opening. As I started to feel awful about the whole thing, one of the two pilots standing below the steps said, "Let's flip her on her side." So, Dad and the EMTs carefully rolled me onto my left side. Now one EMT was positioned directly in front of my face, cradling my upper body like a sleeping bag, while my dad and the other EMT supported my plaster-encased legs. I was an arrow with legs for feathers. I'm sure it looked as awkward as it felt. But as the guys slowly guided me through the doorway, there was an audible sigh of relief from all three. I fit!

They carried me straight onto my hospital bed, which was bolted to the plane's floor. The Caterpillar (CAT) nurse and EMTs made sure I was secured into my fancy lie-flat seat. Once my dad, mom, and the nurse took their own seats, I turned to my dad with a slight grin. "At least we know how to get me off the plane now," I said. He shook his head and smiled.

We made it home to the regional Peoria airport, where a second ambulance was waiting on the tarmac to drive us home. Though I was uncomfortable and felt some pain, my whole body relaxed as I rolled through the front door of our house. That first night, my dad placed me in a reclining wheelchair and guided me into the kitchen so I could eat with my family. The problem was, I was too reclined and too rigid to see the plate my mom set on my chest. As we discussed each other's latest thoughts and experiences, one of my family members would tell me where to aim my fork. "The meat is at two o'clock . . . Your potatoes are at ten o'clock." Half the food rolled down my neck and wedged itself in the top of my cast. A couple of peas rolled like a perfect putt into the small, round cutout in my abdomen. I laughed it all off. I was grateful to be sitting at the kitchen table with my loved ones again.

I didn't fully comprehend it in middle school, but the significance of the people who helped me as a young girl was enormous. It wasn't just that they coached, listened, and joined me through some very tough times. I was also seeing strength in its most tangible form—sacrifice. With a very memorable introduction, CAT had become a part of my village before I ever knew I'd spend my career there. Here was the largest earthmoving equipment manufacturer in the world, moving heaven *and* earth to help a girl in a body cast get back home. If the C-suite had simply told my dad he wouldn't lose any vacation days while helping me get home, we'd have considered them very thoughtful. But they entered into our lives and saw a dad who loved his daughter and wasn't afraid to ask for help. I thought a lot about that over the summer, imagining the leaders at CAT who'd allowed us to use the company jet despite the inconvenience and expense. I also smiled about having a dad who was willing to stake his reputation on looking out for his little girl instead of himself.

The conversation he had with his superior couldn't have been an easy one, and though my dad always downplayed it, I know there was a high possibility of rejection. It was a company jet, for Pete's sake! And my dad was not a top executive. Who makes that kind of request when they're not in a position of leverage? A man who is looking at others' needs more than his own.

To this day, I keep a picture under my computer keyboard of me being carried up the steps of that plane. It's there to constantly remind me that looking up to others requires something other than eyesight; it requires personal sacrifice of a kind greater than simply giving up our time and energy for their sake. To truly see others' value, we have to give up our preconceived notions of who they are or appear to be. We have to let go of the premature belief that we have all the necessary facts to form an accurate conclusion.

———

The Little Prince writer, Antoine de Saint-Exupéry, was spot-on when he included in his story the pivotal line "One sees clearly only with the heart. Anything essential is invisible to the eyes."[4] We should ask ourselves whether we believe in the eyes of the heart. Don't we know, deep down, that there is always more to others than meets the eye? Are we willing to do the work required to see what more there is? It's easy to believe that sort of work is tedious or even risky if you suspect you won't like what you find.

To truly see others' value, we have to give up our preconceived notions of who they are or appear to be.

While it's true that not everything we discover about others is beautiful and inspiring, there is always gold too. Besides, aren't hidden treasures the most valuable of all? We don't think much of a common piece of granite, but we rearrange our lives to obtain a diamond. The treasure inside others is even more valuable than that.

CHAPTER 4

THE VALUE OF BEING WRONG—AT FIRST

'd like to think most of us truly believe that every person on this planet is uniquely valuable. But we don't act like it, do we? Do we see everyone we pass as we would someone famous, as if they have something interesting, important, or even indispensable to offer? I know parents see their kids this way. Friends see their closest friends this way. Good leaders see their team members this way. But how do we see the stranger? How do we see the person outside our own orbit, with whom we don't have an obvious bond or to whom we feel we have no obligation? Do we see immeasurable potential when we walk the streets of our cities or the halls of our offices? People—mere people—would intrigue and excite us if we did. We wouldn't find it difficult to enter into others' lives. We'd see it as an adventure, a challenge, a treasure hunt with a reward to be shared. Unfortunately, if you stroll the city streets, this isn't the reality you observe.

Sadly, what we see on a far more regular basis are people passing each other with blinders on. When we do look at one another, there's far more presumption and dread than appreciation and an enthusiasm to know more. How do we flip that script? It starts by each of us refusing to accept the default conclusions our brains provide us. The truth is, to some degree we have to see that we are wrong about others before we can be right.

My parents and I returned to Maryland ten weeks after the plane ride, to have my body cast removed and begin my physical therapy. To get there, my mom asked Bradley University if she could borrow one of their vans. She'd only started working there ten months earlier, but like my dad, she wasn't looking at herself, or at protocol; she was looking up to me. Bradley University said yes, and my dad then MacGyvered my reclining wheelchair to the van floor and drove us to Baltimore. Once there, my parents admitted me to Children's Hospital, where I was to live for the duration of my recovery. The bad news was, my mom and dad could only stay with me for the first two weeks. They both had to get back to work, and while I understood that, it didn't make it any easier. I was still a young girl, battling through all the questions of identity, self-esteem, and desire. The good news was, there were many other little people on my floor doing physical therapy under Dr. Kopits. Their presence was particularly opportune because being at Children's instead of Johns Hopkins taught me that the next level of my growth was learning to see others the way I wanted them to see me—to see beyond what was plain to see.

There was a girl on my floor who permanently lived at Children's. I'll call her Mary. She had a skin condition that was so extreme, it warranted around-the-clock care and a certain degree of isolation. All of her skin was basically one big infection. She had no fingers because the bacteria had eaten away at them, and her skin had been pulled back to her wrists. She didn't have eyelids, so she slept with her eyes open. She had no hair, couldn't walk, and might have weighed twenty-five pounds. A lot of people couldn't bear the sight of her.

There was another girl who lived at Children's full-time whom I'll call Lisa. She'd suffered severe burns over a majority of her body when she was a child. As a result, whatever part of her wasn't covered by a hospital gown was covered in thick mounds of scar tissue. Her nerves from head to toe would frequently shoot sparks of pain throughout her body, and she had somehow learned to cope with it; I've learned since then that the suffering she endured was relentless.

Lisa and Mary were some staggering kind of warriors inside their broken bodies, especially when you consider that neither girl had any family around. Ever. Their home was a room in a Baltimore hospital, and I never once saw anyone visit them besides Dr. Kopits and the nurses.

There were about a dozen LPA comrades who occupied rooms next to Mary and Lisa, so when it came to proximity, we were close. But when it came to comprehending how it felt when people either couldn't look at you or couldn't stop looking at you, we were even closer. We may not have been able to grasp the specifics of their ailments—really, none of us could wholly grasp the specific challenges of any other person on our floor—but we all knew about pain, disappointment, and fear. We may not have known how it felt to not have a home or a family to hold you, but we understood loneliness and feelings of unworthiness. My relationships with Mary and Lisa taught me that empathy isn't dependent on parallel circumstances.

Both quickly became part of our hall's cohort and joined us for full-time shenanigans. The girls on the hall, who comprised the majority, occasionally shut the boys out of one of our rooms and giggled about which ones we thought were cute. We'd swap food and books, and share secrets and fears. Over the course of that shared first summer at Children's, we'd learn that Mary loved the color purple. Her favorite food was cinnamon rolls, and she dreamed of being a veterinarian. Lisa liked all the characters from the *Peanuts* gang, especially Peppermint Patty. She was allergic to bees and could roll her tongue. There was such beauty in our common ground. When I watched *The Goonies* for the first time several years later, that ragtag group of comrades in the film reminded me so much of our clan on the fourth floor. Like Mikey, Chunk, Data, Stef, Sloth, and the others we, too, were discovering treasure. The difference was that our treasure was found in each other and the depth of our relationships. We also had a lot of fun along the way.

I remember one day we noticed how the nurses would pick up the phones and dial a certain number and it would turn the phone system into an intercom throughout the entire hospital. We nominated a couple of spies to get close enough to spot the number pattern the nurses dialed. I was one of them. It was the number 86. We held on to this information for a couple more nights until the time was right to test it out.

At approximately 10:00 p.m., we commandeered the phone in the empty nurses' station in the middle of our hall. Michael was the name of one of the boys in our cohort, and at the time there was a television commercial for Malt-O-Meal where a boy's stomach would say in a deep voice, "Edgar, I'm hungry. I want my Malt-O-Meal." Our Edgar picked up that phone, punched in 86, and announced, "Edgar, this is your tummy. Where's my Malt-O-Meal?"

Our eyes lit up in shock. It worked! We turned to each other, eyeballs like dinner plates, and slapped our hands over our mouths to smother our laughter.

We'd already discussed our exit plan, so we calmed our convulsing giggles as best we could and immediately dispersed from the nurses' station into smaller groups and a more casual manner. *Hanging out in the hallway like usual* . . .

Suddenly, two nurses came rushing into the hall from the kitchen. They looked up and down the hall, trying to make sense of what had happened. It was a bigger deal than we had imagined—the intercom was primarily meant for critical situations, like paging a doctor or requesting additional help—but we kept our cool that night and shrugged our shoulders in innocence when asked if we knew anything. The next morning the head nurse interrogated us for a second time. She called us into the hallway, and with her hands on her hips, she said curtly, "Who did it?" Again, we didn't know *what* she was talking about.

Our nurses were some of the most amazing people who, unfortunately, didn't always get our best behavior. Still, they were as eager as we were to make our floor as lighthearted as humanly possible. At least once a week, they placed us all in one room and handed each person a large syringe without the needle. Then they set a large bucket of water in the middle of the room and let us go after each other with hospital-issue squirt guns. Those suckers could produce some serious water pressure. They were like the original Super Soakers, and we were all drenched within minutes.

While each patient on our hall was there for a serious and sometimes grave reason, from cancer to severe infection to major surgery, moments like these made for an incredibly rare culture that was never devoid of genuine joy and dignity— even in the midst of the darkness that we all knew wasn't far away.

One evening we noticed a deceased person being wheeled on a gurney to the elevator. It wasn't someone from our floor, so a childish detachment set in. The thought popped into my head that there must be a morgue in the building somewhere, and that body was headed there. I rallied the troops later that night for a little field trip.

We waited until after midnight, as the venture would require a little more "free time" than a moment to dial up the intercom. Once the coast was clear, I went door-to-door and waved everyone into the hall. I led our huddle to the elevator, and on a guess, I punched the button to the lowest level. When we stepped out, the entire floor was dark except for the dim fluorescent lights above the hallway in either direction. I led us down the hall to the right, reading the plaques beside each door until we found what we were looking for at the end of the hall. To my unexpected disappointment, the silver plaque to the right of the wide metal door read, simply: "Morgue." I don't know what else I thought it would say; my middle school mind probably hoped for "House of the Dead" or something in the horror genre. I'd built up my defenses in preparation. I'd warned my comrades what we might behold on this journey. And all we had was a plaque with "Morgue" on it. Boring. Then I had the thought that we might as well look around in there. There was no one on the entire hall but us and whoever was inside. I wiggled the handle and tried to enter. The door wouldn't budge. A few more of us tried. No luck. It was locked—of course. But there was a window cut in the top half of the door, and we could see the room was dimly lit from what we'd discover were small, under-cabinet lights that presumably remained on 24/7.

We quickly devised a rotating human ladder that allowed everyone to peer inside. When I looked, I saw nothing but a couple of empty gurneys, medical equipment, and a wall of stacked, handled, rectangular doors. We'd seen enough movies to know what was behind those doors, but no one dared voice it. There was simply an eerie silence as each person took his or her turn. When the last person had had a peek, someone spoke the mind of us all: "I think we should head back."

Over the next five summers, I underwent multiple surgeries and rounds of therapy in Baltimore—on my hips, my knees, and my ankles. I saw some of the same kids each summer. I met new ones. I formed lifelong bonds. And I learned how to say permanent goodbyes. As much as I missed my parents' presence during those seasons, I felt at home at Children's; my hallmates were an extension of my family, and they colored my most vivid adolescent memories. I was always proud to introduce them to my parents when they returned to bring me home.

• • •

In contrast to my mom's calm demeanor and thin figure, my dad had a commanding presence and a sturdy, six-foot-two frame. He kept a thick head of brown hair his whole life. He was like a blue-collar Tom Selleck, but a little thicker and without the Hollywood glitz. His face was pleasant, even when stern, and people always took notice when he entered a room or opened his mouth to speak. His deep voice and unhurried mannerisms made you feel safe in his presence—especially if you were a kid. He was a benevolent bear around us patients, and everyone fell in love with him. Dad regularly did "rounds" through our hall, visiting each of my hospital mates. He learned everyone's breakfast order from McDonald's in a matter of two days and showed up every morning thereafter with several white, red, and yellow bags full of Egg McMuffins, giant pancakes, hash browns, and apple pies. He was also the king of knock-knock jokes—a few of which even elevated beyond dad-joke realm—and he was the unofficial welcoming committee for the parents of new patients entering physical therapy for the first time. I watched countless quarters magically appear from behind new patients' ears. I'd roll my eyes a thousand times, but inside I was as proud as any daughter in the world.

He never said it outright, but I think being able to offer lightness in the oft-heavy environment of that hospital gave him a sense of purpose. Maybe even some personal redemption. I never doubted my dad's love for me. And though he tried to hide it, I knew he hated seeing me struggle.

My dad was the youngest of six children and spent his

formative years in Tennessee, where his father was often gone chasing down odd jobs, and his mother, to whom he was closest, was the breadwinner. This was during World War II, and to support herself and her kids, his mom worked long hours as a nurse in a local hospital.

When Dad was thirteen, his mother passed away unexpectedly. Shaken but stoic, he went to live with one of his sisters in Tennessee because his father was not in a position to care for him. A year later, a tornado destroyed his sister's home, which left her family in dire straits. Feeling that they could no longer properly care for my dad, his sister and her husband sent him to Peoria to live with one of their older brothers.

When he was just shy of high school graduation, my dad joined the Air Force and wouldn't return to Peoria until his honorable discharge four years later. The summer after he returned, he attended a stock car race with my mom's brother. My mom was driving in the powder puff race. She didn't win, but when she and my dad got one look at each other, the real prize revealed itself. (I still laugh at my mom driving a stock car back then because I've never seen my mom drive above the speed limit.)

If my mom was the heart of our family, my dad was the backbone. And the funny bone. We relied on his strength and consistency, but also his humor. His commanding presence, but also his gentleness. He was the best kind of balance, and that extended to how he fathered us kids. Authoritative, playful, fair, thoughtful. When it came to me, he knew when to step in to help and when to step back and let me have my moment, even if it meant I would learn through failing.

I accepted a daily paper route with my sister during eighth grade, delivering thirteen newspapers throughout our neighborhood. My bike was small and couldn't carry my half in one trip, nor could I have pedaled with the added weight. My dad jimmied two baskets on either side of my bike that could hold a total of four papers. I'd deliver the four and then go back to our house to get the next four papers. Deliver, refill, repeat. I always did my own route except when the snow was deep. Then my dad would deliver them on foot on my behalf. I'd bundle up on the front porch and oversee his aim. (He did great . . . almost always.)

Later, when it came time to get my own car, I visited several dealerships before realizing I needed to recruit my dad to come with me. The same thing kept happening every time I went alone: I'd walk through the door and stand there waiting for a salesperson to come over. Nobody ever came. So, I'd walk to the counter and ask if someone could help me. Hesitantly, they'd send over the most junior person, who'd end up being no help at all, and I would leave after five minutes.

My dad agreed to come along, and of course, when we walked in together, salespeople fell all over themselves. As we toured the lot and inspected the different options, he deferred to me. Did I like the interior? Was there enough trunk space? Did I want to go classic white or navy blue? After the purchase was made and the paperwork was signed for a black cherry Dodge Daytona Turbo, the salesman handed my dad the keys.

"Why are you handing these to me?" he asked, incredulous. "It's her car!"

Getting my own set of wheels came at the perfect time because it coincided with getting my first full-time job at

Caterpillar. After I finished my first year of graduate school, I applied for a summer internship at CAT. I was obviously familiar with the company, not only because they employed my dad and had graciously let me use their jet after my hip surgery, but because it was headquartered in Peoria. Everybody in town was familiar with it, and many families that I knew well worked there too. If I could land a CAT internship, I knew it would look great on my résumé and be a solid career move.

I had by this point learned that my math skills made me well suited for the emerging field of information technology (IT). It was the late 1980s, and there were very few women in the technology field, let alone the specialization of this new thing called the internet. I thrived on the challenge of learning the topic, and then a recruiter at CAT, named Chuck, delivered the disappointing news over the phone that I wasn't accepted for their summer IT internship.

As I was sighing with defeat, he said, "But we'd like to offer you a full-time position instead. That is, if you'd like to work here."

You would have been hard-pressed to find someone more excited than I was. I could barely squeak out a response.

"Really?" I said. "Really?"

Over the next twenty years, I built an extremely fulfilling career at CAT, holding different positions in various divisions. When I made the jump to its philanthropic arm, the Caterpillar Foundation, in 2011, my primary role became leading a team in investing millions of dollars in grant money every year to create sustainable change in individual lives. Of all the facets of my job that I loved—the collaboration, strategy, research, advocacy—it was the fostering of relationships with both our grantees and the individuals they were helping that I treasured most of all. It often reminded me of my summers at Children's and my relationships with both the medical staff and my fellow patients.

In 2013, I traveled to Uganda with one of those grantees, Opportunity International (OI), which provides small business loans, insurance, and savings accounts in underdeveloped countries. It was a typical muggy day as we headed east from Kampala. The dirt roads made for a long and bumpy ride, and I lasted an hour before I needed to use the ladies' room, also known where we were as "the bush." The driver pulled off the road in an area with good coverage. I had no toilet paper, but that wasn't remotely a concern. I walked about ten feet from the vehicle and realized that if a black mamba were to strike my backside when I squatted, my colleagues might never find me. The dry grass was over my head. Needless to say, I survived, while providing some comic relief to my fellow travelers. I felt as though I should probably bow when I finally returned to the Land Cruiser.

Two hours later down the dirt road, we finally arrived at the village I'd come to Africa to see. We pulled off the road into a (shorter) grassy opening. I approached a group of fifty farmers who were OI clients. I was there to hear their stories and learn how our investments in their work were helping their families overcome generations of poverty. OI used GPS mapping to determine the precise size of the farmers' land so they could maximize their plantings, then arranged training so they could determine the ideal blend of seed and fertilizer that would yield the biggest harvest. This sort of information is provided on the labels of the plants we buy at our local

Home Depot, but these farmers historically relied on a blend of trial and error and local assumptions. Though it's not bad information, it's rarely complete. Through our partnership, we were able to give them the broader understanding they needed.

Out of the group of about fifty farmers, a woman named Betty stood out. Her yellow cotton dress, which was probably a far more vibrant shade before the years of sun and layers of dirt infiltrated every last fiber, was like a high five among the earth tones of the others' clothing. I saw it in my peripheral vision the whole time I spoke to the group.

When I finally approached her and introduced myself, she responded vibrantly, telling me her name. I asked her if she'd like to sit and talk with me, and I pointed to a tree that cast a large shadow where we could find some refuge from the heat. She nodded and waited for me to lead the way.

We spent ten minutes together, and her strength seemed to grow with each passing minute. She shared with me how her husband had been significantly injured and could no longer run their sugarcane farm. She successfully took over and kept her family afloat. But she had bigger aspirations than her family's survival. Her parents couldn't afford to send her to school, so her dream was to ensure all ten of her kids attended college and could support themselves and their families with good-paying careers in a bigger city, like Kampala.

As she spoke, I thought back to when I started at Caterpillar in the late 1980s. It was an overtly masculine brand in the male-dominated construction industry, and I was eager to prove myself worthy of the fraternity. I knew the task would not be easy. Betty and I had far different circumstances, but there were threads of her story that I couldn't help but relate to—not just on a female level, but on a human level. The more I saw her, really saw her, the more empowered I felt by her presence. She was a gift to me. A treasure.

You might assume my capacity for empathy and compassion came from my own situation. The truth is, it came from the people in my life who first showed it to me. People like Dr. Kopits. The LPA community. My family. As I grew from an uncertain middle schooler to a young adult, they taught me the value of a steady support system and the power one's perspective had on another's life. Their ability to see beyond my stature, my voice, my age, into the strength and potential in my soul—that's what shaped the way I saw others, like Mary and Lisa, and later, Betty. It made me realize that, sure, I looked different and I sounded different, but I faced adversity and dreamed like everyone did—even my first hospital roommate, Alana, who at seventeen lost her leg to cancer, and at eighteen lost her life. She suffered big. But she dreamed bigger, dreamed of attending college, having a boyfriend, and one day getting married. Had I not taken the time to know her—to peer beyond her unfortunate realities right in front of me—I'd have never discovered her bright, brilliant soul. I'd have never been lifted up by her mere presence. At most, I'd have felt sorry for her. I'd have been capable of sympathy but not empathy. Information but not understanding.

What would happen if we all sought to know each other beyond first sight? Peer beyond the initial snapshot? What if we met others with the primary objective to seek out our similarities and our shared battles? With the goal of discovering the differences between us that can educate and expand our understanding of ourselves, the world, life itself? What if we allowed our shared humanity to be the doorway, letting that be enough and not waiting for a more elaborate invitation to enter in?

Because we live in a world that frequently rewards us for looking a certain way, we're often punished—whether it's being bullied or teased or overlooked—for not measuring up to certain physical standards. However, in our hearts I think most of us know that the real measure of any person has little to do with what can be gauged by a lens, ruler, or scale. To see a person's real worth, and to help him or her see it too, we have to grow beyond a reliance on visual cues like height and weight or skin color or clothing labels.

Visual data is not the sum of any person. Operating by that strategy is no different from seeing a picture of someone and concluding you know him. It never works. How often have you seen a photo of someone and thought one thing, and then met the person only to discover that she was entirely different than you expected? While some of us like being right about a person—like being perceived as a good judge of character—and even stake our identities on that perceived strength, let's stop that nonsense. Let's strive for a higher standard than that. The greatest leaders in history didn't judge books by their covers.

Nelson Mandela, Mother Teresa, Rosa Parks, and other world changers didn't reach their accomplishments because they were good at judging character. They changed the world because they saw beyond stereotypes and snap judgments to the astounding value in every person. They were actually good at judging possibility. They were so amazed by the potential they could see in others that they fought for individual value to their own detriment, and they taught others to do the same. In some instances, they taught entire countries to see differently.

Have you ever considered why you are so moved by under-dog stories? There are few surprises more fulfilling than an unexpected hero rising up and coming through. *Les Misérables* is not one of the greatest stories ever written because a super-hero wins despite adversity. It's the story of an impoverished thief who is scorned and imprisoned by society but seen, really seen, by one man, Bishop Myriel. How the bishop sees Jean Valjean changes the way Jean begins seeing others, and alters the course of his life. Jean fulfills his potential as his eye for the inherent value in others steadily improves, this ability eventually becoming so second nature that he's able to see his greatest adversary through the lens of grace and worthiness.

They changed the world because they saw beyond stereotypes and snap judgments to the astounding value in every person.

You and I are walking among unexpected heroes every day, everywhere we go. We can see them if we choose to see them. And for those who don't yet see themselves, we can help them see. The trouble is, we have an addiction to being right about each other. The addiction is nothing more than a safety net for our own insecurities, but we don't see it that way. We wear being right about someone as a badge. It's time we see the greater value in being wrong about people.

What if instead of assuming we know enough about the people around us, we begin assuming we don't know enough? What if instead of trying to prove we're right about others, we set out to discover how we're wonderfully wrong? Will we be disappointed by others? Of course. But there is no way to make a deep, lasting impact in the lives of others by preempting disappointment. The only thing we should aim to be right about is that another person was worthy of our attention and had great potential. The path to impact in others' lives begins when our perspective on them is focused on their transformation, not our own vindication.

CHAPTER 5

LETTING DOWN YOUR GUARD

We tend to see others' problems more readily than we see their value because, as I said in the introduction, our brains are prewired to spot threats to our own safety and comfort. Sometimes we refer to this tendency as "having our guard up." How quickly does your guard go up when you're in the presence of someone new? As a young girl who was increasingly smaller than her peers, I put my guard up almost immediately upon meeting a new person. Was he going to look at me funny? Was she going to point a finger and laugh? Was that person over there going to be the next one to shove me down?

For a time, asking me to focus on others' value felt like asking me to step into the lion enclosure at the zoo and see how beautiful the giant beast's mane is. It took a timely relationship with an amazing nurse to teach me that when I was on the defense, I only perceived others' problems, issues, and shortcomings. It was impossible to spot their value or the positive results that could ensue with them if all I saw was a possible threat.

Kathy was a nursing student assigned to me during my two hip surgeries at Hopkins that first summer. She was twenty years old to my thirteen, which put her in the category of supercool older sister. But she became much more than that. She offered me a tangible example of a person who focused on positive results with others rather than on their problems.

Part of me wants to say that Kathy was no one special—which is what she would say—but that wouldn't come across as I intend. What I mean is that when we met, she hadn't just concluded six months in prayer and silence at a monastery. She hadn't been raised in a convent or sat for a decade in the calming presence of a yogi. (She's cackling loudly at this, I'm sure.) She was the opposite of all that, in the very best way. Kathy was a tall, direct, strong-willed northeasterner who didn't hoard her strength. She gave it away, breathed her confidence and might into whoever was with her. In her presence you could feel her strength pulsing through your body like some sort of magical menthol.

Kathy interpreted pain and hardship differently than most. In her view, they were an inevitable part of life and, therefore, common. So common, in fact, that there was no reason to dance around another's adversity, wondering what to say or do to avoid offense; doing so only delays your ability to lighten another's load. Her philosophy was, get in there and help. I was taken in by her from the beginning.

She'd say she was a kid when we met that first summer at Johns Hopkins. That's not true. Kathy was wise beyond her years, and there was a reason. She was the classic oldest child of an adult alcoholic. However, she wasn't the oldest. Her brother, who was one year older, responded to their father's chaos by wrecking cars. The role of stabilizer fell to Kathy. She didn't run from the role. Her mom was willful and loving but often consumed with the baggage of her husband's addiction. Kathy became the de facto alpha of her family at twelve years old, and consequently she carried a strained relationship with her father until his death. She was mentored largely by her circumstances and advanced discernment; they goaded her into a young maturity that grew thick skin over her soft complexion. But her heart somehow remained supple.

After my first hip surgery, the initial few nights felt long and miserable. I was immobile from the chest down, which made the homesick loneliness I felt slightly more bearable because my needs were met by others around the clock. I was never by myself for very long. Of course, the nights were even longer for my parents, especially my mom, who slept on an old, wooden cot next to my bed. Kathy was responsible for me for ten successive days. Having come out of two ten-hour surgeries in seven days, I was glad to be bound to a hospital bed but, to my chagrin, there is no toilet in a hospital bed, even though one still has to use the bathroom. I'll save you the details of the daily humiliation except to remind you that I was in a body cast. While Dr. Kopits was kind enough to carve an opening in my cast where it was needed most, I couldn't transport myself to the toilet, sit down, or wipe myself. However, Kathy could. This will sound funny, but her been-there-done-that attitude was a tremendous blessing. She was neither surprised by the job nor particularly moved by it. With her it was always, "All right, let's get this done, Michele." I can't imagine if she had been emotional about it. I'm sure I would have chosen to mess myself rather than compound my discomfort with hers.

After two weeks of an undesirable sort of bonding, I was released to go home until my hips had healed enough to have my casts removed and begin my physical therapy. You already know about the private jet ride home that almost didn't happen. What I didn't tell you was that right before I was discharged from Johns Hopkins, Kathy scribbled her home phone number on the back of a prescription note and handed it to my mom. "Call me when you come back for physical therapy," she said.

It was a thoughtful gesture. My mom thanked her and we said our goodbyes. We hadn't guessed that Kathy meant for us to actually call her. When we returned to Baltimore six weeks later, my mom and I discussed whether Kathy would even remember us.

"She sees so many people, Mom," I pointed out. "I doubt she'll even remember our names."

"It can't hurt to try," my mom replied. She picked up the phone in my hospital room and dialed the number.

What happened next wasn't a dramatic movie scene, and you won't need tissues. But before I tell you what ensued, I should tell you that Kathy grew up in a rural part of Howard County, Maryland. Farmland, mainly, where there was no ethnic diversity whatsoever and certainly not a little person anywhere in sight. Before Kathy had met me at Hopkins six weeks earlier, she'd never seen a person with dwarfism. Had

I known this, I would have been confident that Kathy was being dutiful by passing along her number. I might have even felt that I made her a little uncomfortable (even if it didn't seem that way when we were together). My point is, I probably would've begged my mom not to call her. "Mom," I might have said, "she was just being nice, but she doesn't want to hang out with me any more than she has to." I would've been dead wrong about her and not known it. Fortunately, it never came to that.

My stay in Baltimore was going to be six weeks long this time around, and I wouldn't be at Johns Hopkins. That was another deterrent to calling Kathy. I wouldn't be at the hospital where she was studying and putting in her hours. I'd be in a room at Children's Hospital a few miles away, where the rehab facilities were located. When the phone rang for the fourth time, my mom looked at me and shrugged. Then Kathy picked up. She was out of breath as she said hello.

"Hello, Kathy," my mom began. "I don't know if you remember us, but this is Mrs. Sullivan, Michele Sullivan's m—"

"Hi!" Kathy interrupted, still panting. "I was hoping you'd call. Are you back in town?"

"We are . . . and, well, we just thought we'd call and say hi since we were back. How have you been?"

"I've been great. Sorry I'm so out of breath; I'm running a little late for class and trying to get my act together."

"Oh, I'm very sorry. I'll let you—"

"Is Michele checked in to her room at Children's?"

"Yes, she is. We're here now."

"I'll come by when I'm out of class. Is that okay? What room are you in?"

My mom walked over to the door to verify the number and relayed it to Kathy.

"Got it. I'll be there a little after lunch. Where are *you* staying, Mrs. Sullivan?"

"In a hotel nearby," my mom said.

"Don't stay in a hotel. Come stay here with me at my parents' house."

My mom thanked her for offering but insisted she'd stay in a hotel. She was already checked in, she explained, and my dad was coming in two days, and they'd be an imposition on her family.

A battle of wills ensued, until finally, my mom gave in. There was plenty of room, Kathy said, and her mom would enjoy their company.

That accommodating strangers would be "enjoyable" is the hospitable thing to say, but my mom wasn't buying it and was still bent on not being a burden. When she hung up the phone, she told me that we would eat our dinners out each night, and eat daytime meals at the hospital. The only thing she'd do at Kathy's house was sleep. That plan didn't last twenty-four hours.

On our first night in Maryland, Kathy's mother invited us to dinner and served up a pot roast with peas, carrots, and mashed potatoes. Over dinner my mother learned that Kathy's dad was no longer living in the home. He'd left them two years before. That evening, our mothers sat up late at the kitchen table, sharing a cup of decaf and talking about their families' challenges. Marrying an alcoholic husband and raising a disabled child are not the same thing by a long shot, but the experiences had common threads that touched the part of our hearts that hates seeing a loved one struggle. Our moms bonded that night.

When my dad arrived two days later, the bond between our families deepened—over poker. Kathy's mom pulled a deck of cards from a kitchen drawer, and my dad's eyes lit up. They were both fanatics. They sat at the kitchen table every night thereafter, trying to prod each other into a tell, but neither liked losing. I sat in the adjacent family room while my mom read and Kathy studied. With no one to talk to, I regularly tuned in to my dad's poker match and giggled at the outbursts after a hand had turned against one of them. Every once in a while, I'd glance over at my mom and catch the corners of her mouth rising upward. She preferred a quieter relaxation, but I knew she, like Kathy's mom and me, relished the jovial presence of my dad.

This became the routine for my parents' first weeklong stay in Baltimore, and every stay thereafter for the next five years. A home-cooked meal with Kathy and her mom, followed by cards at the table for the fierce competitors, and downtime in the family room for Mom and me. We'd keep our routine, even on nights when Kathy was working at Hopkins. Afterward, my parents would tuck themselves into bed in the guest room, which was eventually renamed "the Sullivan room." They began leaving clothes in the closet and dresser to lighten the load for the next visit.

On a few occasions we did break tradition and eat out. My dad insisted on contributing somehow, and paying for dinner was one way. It was the least he could do, he'd say, and the fresh air would do us good. One night, we went for crab cakes. They are a specialty of Maryland, and the best places for them are century-old converted boathouses featuring all manner of candid photos peppering the walls, checkered tablecloths over wooden tables, and a well-stocked bar. We enjoyed a lazy, long dinner, and my dad lost count of his beers. He wasn't much of a drinker, except socially now and then, so his big size didn't help much. When the five of us returned to the house, he promptly brushed his teeth with a red-and-white tube of Brylcreem, a hair product. He made enough of a ruckus rinsing, spitting, and laughing, that Kathy's mom asked from the hallway what had happened, and my dad confessed. "For Christ's sake, Don!" she exclaimed. It was her standard, oft-fitting outburst. It always seemed to make us laugh. This was the fun-loving, unpredictable effect my dad had, so I wasn't surprised when Kathy told me at the hospital one day that she was grateful to see her mom smiling so much.

There was an easy delight that came when our families were together. Over five years and many weeklong visits, we became so close there was no more "our family" and "their family." We were close relatives. We were also more than that. Looking back, I think each family needed the fresh air the other provided during that season, for different reasons. While we never said it, we were each other's answer to prayer. More specifically though, Kathy was like my guardian angel, and I was her sidekick.

My parents couldn't remain in Baltimore indefinitely. My mom's work at Bradley University and my dad's at Caterpillar required them to come and go, often leaving me at Children's by myself for weeks at a time. When they weren't around, I had my comrades at Children's, and I had Kathy. Or maybe it's more accurate to say that she had me.

When my parents were back in Peoria, Kathy's visits didn't wane; they increased. She'd drop by to chat over homemade chocolate chip cookies. She'd get permission to administer the antinausea shots that she knew I needed right after a surgery. She'd even "kidnap" me and drive me—body cast and all—to her mom's house, where she'd lay me on the green kitchen counter. She'd then take a seat on an adjacent barstool and do her homework. I didn't mind. It was everything to have her want me there. We'd often talk between her studying spells, and I'd ask her about college and boys and everything I ever wanted to ask an older sister but was too scared to ask my mom.

She'd answer honestly, sometimes pensively when she was unsure, but always in unpolished candor. I ate up every word. Now, here's the point where I confess that I was not the easiest teen to have around. Despite my condition and despite my various forms of immobility, I managed to be what Kathy called a "megaphone mouth." It's hard for me to imagine that my squeaky voice could ever be compared to a megaphone, but I will admit, I was adept at being the squeakiest wheel when necessary. I often considered myself the knower of all things medical and would regularly argue with Kathy and Dr. Kopits about the best plan of action for my recovery. This included taking the debates to Kathy's kitchen counter and, when the time was right, raising my point from flat on my back. She was patient with me until it was clear I wasn't going to quit. But she was unbreakable.

I wasn't in the hurry she and Dr. Kopits always seemed to be in, and of course I had no concept of the effects of things like scar tissue and atrophy. I fought the two of them with the conviction of a heavyweight champ until either a compromise was reached or they flat out refused to continue listening to me. Dr. Kopits would gently say, "I'll give that some thought, Michele," and walk out of my room with a vague promise to return "in a little bit." Kathy would stare at me with her eyebrows raised and her hands on her hips. She had me there, as I was often wholly dependent on her to meet my basic needs. I was literally all mouth, and she knew it. I never seemed to scare her away. If anything, my outbursts drew us closer. As annoying as I sometimes was, I think she appreciated the fight in me.

On one occasion, Kathy decided to take me, my roommate Alana, and one more of our floormates to lunch at a place called Ponderosa, one of those serve-yourself buffet restaurants. I'm sure you can imagine the looks when Kathy led three seriously disabled kids into the restaurant. I was in a reclining wheelchair, like a mannequin on a hand truck. Our floormate had a degenerative muscular disease and was permanently bound to a motorized wheelchair. Alana had had her leg amputated earlier that summer, and she was using crutches instead of wearing her prosthetic. How we got through that lunch without a disaster, I'm not exactly sure, but I do know we laughed a lot. Wherever I went with Kathy, there seemed to be a protective bubble around us that shielded me from the reactions of those nearby. She was always herself and seemed quite oblivious to what others might think of her. In a way, she thrived in this environment. As a result, so did those of us with her. When Kathy began loading me back in the car after lunch I screamed, "*Help! Somebody help me! Help!*" like she was kidnapping me. The parking lot was full from the lunch rush, so people were around. "Shut. Up!" she whispered gruffly. "Shut. Up. Michele." Her gentle manner of cradling me into the back seat immediately shifted to something like being one-two-three swung into a pool. Of course, my friends and I were laughing.

Kathy's never been one to back down from something uncomfortable, including a thirteen-year-old loudmouth accusing her of kidnapping. Her initiative kept things lively, for sure, but it was a godsend when things were tough. In that season of life, adversity was always on the daily menu, and not just my own.

When my mom would take a break, Kathy was often the only person with me when I was vomiting for days after the latest surgery. She'd hold the bucket until I was done and then promptly clean up where I'd missed. She wouldn't clean herself until I was spotless. She'd also break protocol and sneak me snacks when other nurses weren't looking. Keep in mind that Kathy wasn't yet finished with nursing school when I met her, so she wasn't doing things that merely could have gotten her kicked out of school. She was doing things that could have derailed her entire career. I'm certain, looking back now, that her colleagues turned a blind eye now and then. We can all appreciate someone who's willing to bend the rules for good reason.

When Alana's cancer returned shortly after her leg was taken, it was Kathy who volunteered to step in and offer her around-the-clock care, especially when it was clear Alana was dying. Kathy was in the final semester of nursing school, and this wasn't a prerequisite for graduating. She knew Alana's cancer had taken over her body. It wasn't the time to step back.

Alana's doctor agreed to move her home, where she'd be more comfortable. Her parents didn't want to hear it, as no parents would, but this was the beginning of hospice care. Kathy moved into the family's house and slept in Alana's room with her for the final six weeks of her life. The only time she was not by Alana's side was when she was in class. It was the only span of time in five years when Kathy wasn't by my side. But I knew where she was, and I wanted her to be there.

Now knowing what you do about her, it probably won't surprise you to hear that Kathy went on to become an amazing pediatric nurse, then a labor and delivery nurse, and then a hospice nurse. She's sixty years old now and still making an impact. Today, she's the nurse who gets the call when an expectant mother is told her unborn child has a condition that will not allow him or her to survive long outside the womb. Kathy is there for the delivery, and she remains with the parents and baby to the very end, which is usually no longer than a few weeks, and sometimes only minutes after birth.

Impact doesn't require something spectacular. Moving toward another can be a direct acknowledgment of his or her value; it can also elevate our own.

There are a few people besides my parents that I'd call personal heroes, and Kathy is one of them. During the most formative five years of my life, when I was no longer growing physically but still searching for ways to grow, Kathy was a model of the profound impact one individual can have on another, by taking initiative in the relationship— saying yes, stepping forward, offering a hand, and focusing on results, not problems. She taught me that impact doesn't require something spectacular. Moving toward another can be a direct acknowledgment of his or her value; it can also elevate our own. It was a lesson I'd carry with me into adulthood, and particularly into my first position at CAT, where examples like Kathy were not always nearby. Fortunately, between Kathy and CAT, I had a little practice.

Hello, world!

Pushing my big brother around

YES! Santa came!

My family—thank you, God!

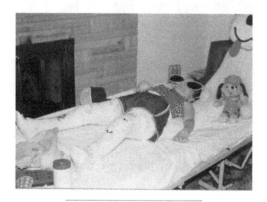

This is how I spent my summer vacation.

I got swept off my feet.

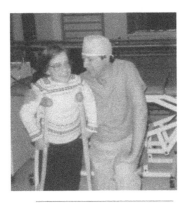

Dr. Kopits impacted so many people, including me.

I love you, Mom and Kathy. Would not be who
I am without your love and support.

MBA graduation day. Couldn't have done it without my mom
and dad. Thank you, God, for blessing me in so many ways.

Meet Mad Dog, the koala bear

So how did they build the pyramids? We couldn't figure it out.

Always wanted a halo, but not this kind!

I wanted to check out a new Caterpillar D11 bulldozer.
That little dot in front of the bucket is me.

Driving around on a Caterpillar backhoe

Doug Oberhelman, Caterpillar CEO, after
completing the water walk at CONEXPO

Thank you, Billy Barty, for starting the Little
People of American organization.

Hervé photo opp at a Little People of America convention

Some of the amazing kids I met in Uganda

Betty, from Uganda, one of the bravest
women I have ever met. God bless.

I love the Faraja students and school in Tanzania.

Dave & Joann Tolmie at Faraja School graduation in Tanzania

With Matt Damon and Gary White of Water.org

Look who I'm looking up to—former president Barack Obama.

Words cannot express my thoughts while meeting Pope Francis in New York.

Me and Bono, one of the most genuinely caring people I know

CHAPTER 6

MAKE THE FIRST MOVE

I've found that it's one thing to believe that everyone has value but it's an entirely different thing to live day to day like it's true. The litmus test for where you stand on the principle is what you do with strangers and the people around you who don't think, look, or act like you do. If you make the first move toward such people in an effort to get to know them, you not only embody the principle that everyone has value, you also find that the value is always there. I realize this discovery is more difficult when the other person isn't receptive to your initiative. This doesn't make the principle less true. It just means you have a little more work to do.

By my teens, I'd played in a couple of school chess tournaments and done well against kids older than me. Then my parents started entering me in tournaments in and around Peoria. While our hometown was far enough from Chicago— about a two-and-a-half-hour drive—that it wasn't amid a major metropolis, the nonschool tournaments were still nerve-racking events for me. The staring and finger-pointing were a given, and name-calling was intermittent. I expected it all at this point, but I never looked forward to it. Then my parents entered me in the Peoria city tournament. Kids from dozens of schools converged at the downtown civic center to compete at one of three age levels. I was in the junior division.

The kids from my school bussed into downtown on a Saturday morning, and the comfort of their familiar presence was quickly erased when I stepped into the huge ballroom where the tournament was to take place. I froze at the sight of dozens of tables spread everywhere and set with chessboards and two stools each. I gazed up at the ceiling some thirty feet above my four-foot body. When I finally let my eyes focus on the unfamiliar people milling around, hundreds of them, I spotted the familiar sights: raised eyebrows, whispers over half-covered mouths, index fingers aimed at me. I tried to remember I was good at chess. Maybe I would win some matches?

My competitor was a boy my age. When I walked up to the table, it was eye level. The seat of my stool was chest high. I stared at it for a moment. Then I inhaled and started to climb like I was scaling Yosemite's Dawn Wall. I reached across and grabbed the back side of the seat with my left hand and pulled myself up until I could swing my right leg onto the stool. I shimmied the rest of my body up and then slid on my whole stomach onto the seat like a sea lion onto a pool deck. Once I'd summited the stool, I flipped over, sat up, and peered across the table at my competition. I immediately realized I was looking through the chess pieces. I worried whether I could even reach all the pieces on the board. I swung my legs to one side and used the table to prop myself up so I could sit on my knees.

I looked back across the table at the boy, and this time he was laughing.

"Hello," I said with a confident smile. "I'm Michele."

He snickered and said nothing back. Just fuel for the fire in my fingers.

We started the match, and before long I was standing on my stool to reach across the table.

"Checkmate," I grunted as I stretched to move my piece into victory position.

It had taken fifteen minutes. When the boy realized what had happened, his face turned bright red. I didn't know if he was angry or embarrassed or both. I didn't ask.

I sat back in my seat and smiled at him. "Good game," I said. "Again, I'm Michele."

He was fuming as I slid off my stool and began walking to the scorer's table. I waited for her to notice me. Like the chess table, her table was also eye level. Every time she looked up, she'd look right over my head. Eventually, I waved my hand and said, "Hello. Hello."

Her head jerked back in shock.

"Honey," she said, "you need to go play your game."

"I did," I replied. "I won."

"No, no, you couldn't be done yet, honey. You need to go find your table and play the game."

"I did," I repeated. "I won. I played at table twelve, and I'm done."

She sat there a moment, clearly stunned and unable to process.

"You're done?"

"Yes, I'm done. Could you tell me what table is next?"

She stared at me a moment more; then she looked down at her paperwork and traced the table assignments with her finger. Table five was next. She still looked troubled as I thanked her and walked away.

I waited near the next table for the previous match to finish—another twenty minutes. Once the previous player had hopped off, I started my second climb onto the stool. Again, my opponent was a boy, and again he giggled. I introduced myself as I had before. Again, it was over quickly. This same scene played out two more times until I reached the fifth and final match—the championship. There were few girls in the tournament, so once again I faced another boy. I suspect that because he knew I was undefeated going into the match, he didn't giggle like the others. Maybe he assumed I was a formidable opponent. We started the match, and I knew right away this one would not end quickly, like the others. We were evenly matched. A crowd had circled around us and was watching as we battled wit against wit. He was very good, and I knew I couldn't waste a single move. As chess goes, one wrong move can lose the game. I was patient. Eventually, he made a mistake. Two moves later I checkmated him.

Something changed in the air the moment I won. It was truly visceral. It was also audible. The crowd noise ramped up, like an hour into a cocktail party, after everyone's had a couple of drinks. The buzz remained as it came time for trophy presentations, and then, like we do when an emcee is about to take the stage, people started shushing each other. By the time they announced my name, you could hear a pin drop. I felt everyone's eyes on me as I hurried down the aisle and took the stage. But this time was different. For the first time they weren't staring only because I was little. They were staring because I was little and I'd still won.

I was handed the trophy—nearly as big as me—and the audience applauded. It was my first trophy, but more important, it implanted in my soul the profound power I had in changing others' perceptions of me through my actions. I'd accepted that I couldn't make myself look different. I couldn't stretch my limbs or hide my height with four-inch heels. But I could do something that elevated others' view of me. I knew by then that people wouldn't naturally move toward me; that didn't mean I couldn't move toward them. Finally, it hit me what my mom had meant when she kept telling me to make the first move.

From that day forward, whenever I walked into a chess tournament, the kids remembered me and would come up to say hi. I remember one instance when a younger boy walked up with his mom.

"This is the girl that won the whole tournament a few months ago," he announced excitedly.

I could tell by the mom's surprised look that he hadn't told her I was little. He'd told her that I'd won.

A few years later, when the CAT recruiter named Chuck hired me, he was demonstrating the same sort of initiative I'd practiced at that chess tournament. By offering a position at a male-dominated company to a twenty-two-year-old woman with a disability, he was clearly not afraid to make the first move. I came to find he wasn't the exception there either. Caterpillar's leadership bred a culture where every person had something to offer; it wasn't just mission-statement lip service that was framed on a waiting room wall. This meant that while I didn't fit the mold at CAT, I was still among people with whom I could thrive. This isn't to say we didn't have bad days.

On my first day of work, I struggled to find a parking spot close to the building. These legs only carry me so fast, and by that I mean I'm more sloth than cheetah. Sensing the time ticking away and not wanting to be late on my first day, I gave up weaving through the parking lot aisles and pulled into the drop-off circle and called it good. The concierge saw me doing it, and once I stepped inside, she scolded me.

"Well, we can't have you doing that again," she asserted. "It's not allowed."

I smiled and said okay.

"Let's get your picture taken then," she said.

I moved backward two steps from her desk. It was all so thrilling—I was about to get my first employee badge!

"I can't see you," she said dryly from behind the camera.

"Hang on," I replied. I'd been to the DMV before, and numerous hotel front desks. I knew how this worked. I stepped back three more paces. There. A better angle now.

"Still can't see you," she said with the emotion of a napkin.

At this point it became another game of chess to me. I looked around and spotted a chair. I slid it into place. Success! The concierge snapped the photo and handed me my new badge.

Next challenge: the turnstile.

I clipped my badge onto my blouse and strutted toward the glistening aluminum gates between me and my new career.

When I reached them, I noticed that the highest turnstile arm came to my neck. Geez. I put both hands on it and shoved. It didn't budge. I couldn't get my weight behind it. I looked back at the receptionist and she was watching me. I smiled and tried once more. No luck. I paused, took a breath, and subtly nodded to myself. I then ducked under the high arm while straddling the low one and kept on walking. I was giggling to myself as I imagined the look on the concierge's face.

Working for Caterpillar was a dream come true, but it wasn't without challenges that required more finesse than physicality. On a Wednesday, four years into my career at Caterpillar, I was called into my division manager's office and told I was being moved laterally to another group. It took me by surprise. I asked why. She only said that's what they needed to do. As I asked more questions I realized, without her saying it, that the move was to a group that wasn't relocating to the company headquarters, as my current group was. What it came down to was that instead of working out accessibility in the HQ building, they were transferring me to another team so they didn't have to deal with it.

I stared at her and held my tongue. I couldn't believe that my career path was based on my disabilities and not my abilities. I walked out and couldn't concentrate the rest of the day.

That night I lamented to my parents. They reminded me that if I didn't stand up now, others' perspectives would not change. The next morning, I asked for a meeting with my manager and the facility manager. I asked point-blank if my move to another group was related to my current group moving to the HQ, which was not set up for disabled access. They hemmed and hawed, and eventually the facility manager admitted it. He was angry by this time and not hiding his feelings. I told them both I didn't think it was right to move me to a different group because they didn't think the building was suitable for me. The facility manager wasn't backing down. "This is ridiculous," he blurted out as he stiffened in his seat. I looked at my manager.

"I'm not moving to another group," I insisted. "I'm moving to the HQ with my current group."

She looked at me a moment, blinked twice, then nodded. She turned to the facility manager. "She's moving to the headquarters with her group. Please work out the parking situation for her."

The facility manager was so irate that he shoved back his chair and stormed out.

My manager worked with him over the next week, and I was given a parking spot in the loading dock area of the building. I was so relieved. From that day forward, the facility manager never acknowledged me when he saw me in the HQ building. However, he did have to respond to me when I sent him a note asking if a lower paper towel holder could be installed in the ladies' room, so I could reach it. I offered to work with him to figure out the height that would work. He wrote nothing back to me, but a couple weeks later I noticed a new paper towel holder had been installed. It was five feet off the floor, like the other one.

I knew Richard, the facilities employee who'd installed the paper towel holder (his boss was the angry one), so when I saw him one day, I asked if he could step into the women's restroom so I could show him something. We giggled at my request, and once the restroom was empty, he followed me in. I walked straight to the new paper towel holder, stood underneath it, and smiled. The bottom of it was a foot over my head. He burst out laughing. Then he apologized for not understanding the situation. Three days later, he reinstalled it at a height I could reach. Richard became a real advocate for me after that day, and we developed a good friendship. His boss, the facilities manager, never did acknowledge me, but I learned that, unfortunately, not everyone wants to see differently. But more do than don't. That was certainly the case at CAT.

Unfortunately, not everyone wants to see differently. But more do than don't.

Initiative became my MO there. In many ways it had to be if I wanted to be seen for more than my disabilities. I've never expected people to ignore my dwarfism. I don't today and I didn't back then. But what I've come to understand is that others aren't responsible for seeing me for *more* than my disabilities. I am. How I behave, how I set the tone, gives others an immediate path to a broader perspective of me. How else will others see me for more than what is obvious?

About a year after the paper towel holder incident, I was on the seventh floor of HQ, where all the executive offices are. I was using my crutches and approaching the corner around which was the elevator. Right before I turned the corner, I overheard an executive ask: "Why the hell did they lower the elevator buttons?"

I waited a few seconds, took a breath, and worked myself around the corner. I approached the executive, who couldn't have known for sure that I'd heard him, and I said hi. He did the same.

"I want to thank you for having someone lower the elevator buttons," I said. "I can reach them now." I placed a hand on the buttons to demonstrate.

"Well," he began with a slight pause, "it was the right thing to do."

A line of advice in Dale Carnegie's classic book *How to Win Friends and Influence People* encourages the reader to always "let the other person save face."[1] In the context in which he presents it, he's referring to not calling out someone's mistake or shortcoming in front of other people. Letting the person save face is about not publicly or directly embarrassing someone because he or she offended you or did something unbecoming, even if the person deserves it. In the book of Proverbs, Israel's third monarch, King Solomon, wrote that it is a person's glory to overlook an offense.[2] I like that way of thinking about it. Said either way, what both he and Carnegie were communicating is that we improve the situation for both parties when we're willing to be the bigger person and not be offended by another person's wrongdoing. It's not easy. But it's the better way, especially when you consider that nobody wins when both parties end up offended.

I think we can also take this approach a step further. In my context, making the first move is based on preempting behavior that's based on assumptions. It's effectively letting another person off the hook before he or she is on the hook. When we take initiative to move toward someone, we often cut off wrong assumptions before they take root and instead allow an interaction to begin on the right foot.

I know what people are thinking when they first see me. I understand that their conclusions are often logical ones. I'm not offended that someone might be a little gun-shy with me. I've been in that situation many times myself, especially recently. My time with the Caterpillar Foundation has given me access to some pretty well-known people. The foundation does a lot of work with Bono's ONE Campaign. I remember the first time I met him. He walked right up to my chair, opened his arms, and leaned down to give me a warm hug and a peck on my cheek. While I certainly didn't have any negative assumptions of him, I hadn't wanted to come across as though I, too, had sold almost 175 million albums or rocked every city in the world over for three decades. Fortunately, I didn't have to overthink my actions or worry about putting my foot in my mouth. He allowed me to save face by making the first move, warmly and genuinely. It instantly elevated my view of him and elevated the path of our relationship from that day forward. Though we're no Bonos (unless you're reading this, B), we can have the exact same effect on others. Celebrity is not a prerequisite for making an immediate impact.

On March 8, 2017, I was in New York City to participate in the largest-ever lobbying event for girls' rights at the United Nations. Organized by ONE as part of their Poverty Is Sexist campaign, the gathering was one of 284 walk-ins around the world *Celebrity is not a prerequisite for making an immediate impact.* to promote gender equality and education for girls who, in many of the world's poorest countries, do not have access to the same opportunities offered to their male counterparts. The Caterpillar Foundation had formally partnered with ONE to meet with the UN deputy secretary-general, Amina Mohammed, and discuss how to better address the struggles girls around the world are facing. My morning began with breakfast at a small restaurant near the UN headquarters on East Forty-Second Street. Seated at my table were a few folks from ONE and three young Nigerian women who had been kidnapped by Boko Haram. They went by the pseudonyms Sa'a, Suzie, and Zai to protect their families in Nigeria. Suzie sat next to me. Sa'a and Zai sat directly across from me.

When the Islamic militant group snatched 276 girls from their beds, I was appalled like everyone, and I followed the story like a hawk. The details were unimaginable. On April 14, 2014, the jihadist group, whose name roughly translates to "Western education is forbidden," had stormed the Government Girls Secondary School in the town of Chibok, Nigeria, where they ambushed the sleeping teenage girls and forced them into truck beds. They'd disappeared into the dark forest minutes after the attack.

The global reaction was immediate. The hashtag #BringBackOurGirls sprang up and spread quickly. When Michelle Obama tweeted a photo of herself holding a sign with the hashtag shortly after the horrific event, the fate of the Chibok girls escalated into the world's consciousness.

In the time since the horrific event, some of the beautiful young ladies have died in captivity; some have given birth; twenty-one have been released, including Sa'a and Zai; and a smaller number, like Suzie, have miraculously escaped. Today, however, there are still approximately 200 young ladies whose fates are unknown. All this in the name of a twisted belief that young ladies shouldn't be educated. Currently, 130 million young ladies around the world are still prevented from receiving an education.

When I sat down next to Suzie, I knew only the larger tragedy into which she'd been forced. I had no idea of her individual story. I quickly introduced myself and told her, Sa'a, and Zai that I was there with the others to bring awareness to their adversity and focus on creating long-term opportunities for young women like them to pursue their full potential. Two of the three wore sunglasses, including Suzie, a choice that characterizes the fear they still feel. They nodded as I spoke but said nothing. I then asked them what they were going to do while in America. Slight smiles came as they each explained that they were attending college on the East Coast; two of them planned to go into medicine. Suzie had plans to pursue a career in law. I told them how impressed I was.

"You must all be very smart," I said, to which they grinned. Then I asked how each of them was able to come to the States. I didn't intend for them to share difficult memories, but I think they could see I was genuinely for them. Suzie spoke first.

She detailed the horrors that she and the others had suffered the night of April 14, 2014. Tears filled my eyes, but I tried to stay strong. She looked down the whole time she spoke. Her voice was somber. Finally, she trailed off. "It wasn't a good situation."

I've been through a lot in my lifetime, but never anything close to what that young lady had to suffer. Part of me wanted to travel straight into the Nigerian bush to rescue the remaining girls. Another part of me wanted to sob. Instead, I summoned strength for Suzie and reached out my hand to hers. She squeezed mine tightly. A couple of tears rolled down my face. I said nothing more. She spoke again and told me that she'd thought night and day about how to escape. She knew it was her only way to survive. Then one evening, when the terrorists were relocating the girls in the backs of trucks, she jumped out and ran. They shot her, but she didn't stop running.

She didn't give any more detail, other than to explain that an organization helped her get back into school and eventually to the US to attend college. She explained that she doesn't just want to practice regular law; she wants to be a lawyer in human rights. She then paused and looked up at me.

"Nobody should go through what we did. I am so happy to see all of you here today."

I still think about that day a lot. I think about Suzie, Sa'a, and Zai. These young ladies are apprehensive, and understandably so. They're afraid for their families back home. The faces of their abducted friends must come to mind multiple times a day. I'm sure it's difficult to hope. It must be a daily challenge to focus their minds and emotions on the tasks before them. They are the bravest young ladies I've ever met. Yet you would never know this by merely looking *at* them.

If you'd seen them on the streets of Manhattan that day, three young ladies among several million, you'd never know they'd just escaped one of the most horrific experiences imaginable. You'd never know that, even in this country, thousands of miles from their captors, they were still anxious everywhere they went. You'd see them wearing sunglasses, outside and inside, and assume it was a fashion statement. You couldn't possibly know they wore them because their self-worth had been shattered and replaced by a profound insecurity that made it difficult to look you in the eyes.

You and I couldn't possibly know any of that, unless we took initiative to introduce ourselves, say hello, and offer a genuine smile, not because we already knew what was inside these beautiful ladies, but because we didn't. And we refused to assume we did.

Seeing further and deeper into the life of another person requires bravery in a different sort of way than we typically think of bravery. Something like cliff diving, for example, requires total self-focus: mind, body, and spirit all in clear, courageous harmony to propel us into the air where we know only birds and planes belong. Propelling ourselves toward someone we don't know requires focus on the other. I think it might even require more courage to do that. We are choosing to transfer our natural focus from ourselves to another person. It's truly a conscious choice but one that can become more natural the more we exercise it. And the more we make the choice, the more others tend to reciprocate it.

There's a particular detail I didn't tell about my Uganda trip, when I first met Betty. The second my colleagues and I stepped out of the van we'd driven from Kampala, a swarm of two dozen children came running over. When they saw me, they stopped dead in their tracks about ten feet from the van. It took me off guard. You'd think I should be used to people looking at me like that. But this was different. As I stood there smiling at them, it struck me that they'd probably never seen a little person, let alone a pasty-white one. I reached out my hand to them and said, "Hi. I'm Michele. What are your names?" The group was stiff and silent. My outstretched hand was equally frozen, like I was a statue. It was awkward at the time, but reliving it now makes me laugh because I am picturing how odd the scene must have looked. Imagine offering your hand to shake a stranger's and leaving it protruding out there like a one-armed mummy for a full minute, with no response from the other person. Fortunately, the first brave child finally stepped up to me, reached her hand toward mine, and revealed a huge, white smile. She told me her name was Ansha, and for about two minutes we talked about what she was studying in school. The floodgates opened.

The other kids immediately began rushing forward to shake my hand and introduce themselves. The next child was a boy who was fascinated with my eight-dollar Avon watch, which shimmered in the African sun. He rubbed it and then exclaimed how beautiful it was, over and over. Others came up and touched my arm or felt my (bottled) blond hair. They were shameless, and I loved it.

I spent the next half hour speaking with the children, fielding their questions: How old was I? *Much older than you.* Where was I from? *A town in America called Peoria.* Soon they all asked the same question in unison as they bounced up and down like human popcorn: Could I please come play with them? Though I knew they didn't realize how limited I was physically—or maybe they did and didn't care—I followed them to a field and played and danced with them as best as I could. There was such joy in their faces, but they couldn't have known how much joy it brought me to be seen in that way. They didn't care that I was short in a strange way they'd never seen before. They didn't care that my skin was a color they'd never seen, and my hair was more like the beards of the goats in the surrounding fields than the curly locks on their heads. They didn't care that I was much older or sported a chair that drove itself. I smiled at them. I was Michele, a playmate, in their eyes.

When my mom told me to get to know others, she was ultimately saying, *You go first. Don't wait for them to come to you, because most people won't.* I've learned that this isn't only my lot in life—it's most people's.

We live in a time when sensitivity to offending other people is high. The spirit of our sensitivities to things like racism, sexism, and bigotry is just. However, we often take it too far when we spend our days either looking for offenses or dialing back interaction with others for fear that we're going to say or do something offensive. It takes courage these days to smile and reach out your hand to someone you don't know, especially someone who seems to fit a certain stereotype that isn't in your comfort zone.

Today's leaders have the selfless courage to move toward people unlike them, people they don't know, even people who evoke a sense of anxiety or fear.

The leaders of today aren't the people who shrink back from interactions and say to themselves, *I don't want to offend,* or *I don't have anything in common with that person.* Today's leaders have more than the cliff-jumping courage required to elevate their own platforms. Today's leaders have the selfless courage to move toward people unlike them, people they don't know, even people who evoke a sense of anxiety or fear.

C. S. Lewis is often credited for a quote that goes something like, "Humility isn't thinking less of yourself; it's thinking of yourself less." It's a great line, but Lewis didn't actually say it. What he actually wrote is, I think, more powerful: "Do not imagine that if you meet a really humble man he will be what most people call 'humble' nowadays: he will not be a sort of greasy, smarmy person, who is always telling you that, of course, he is nobody. Probably all you will think about him is that he seemed a cheerful, intelligent chap who took a real interest in what *you* said to *him* . . . He will not be thinking about humility: he will not be thinking about himself at all."[3]

Making the first move isn't easy. Remember: our default is self-preservation. This is the permanent first hurdle we have to overcome. Because if we all make self-preservation the number one priority, then we won't get very far together. We'll play the games we play to make each other feel seen and valued, but progress will always stall when collective self-sacrifice is required. We will become fractured the minute what I need is different from what you need. What if we stopped playing that game?

There is no doubt that democracy is one of humanity's greatest ideals. It's critical that we don't all think alike. For every "This is how it's done," there should be a "But what about this way?" However, when it comes to thriving relationships, partnerships, and collaborations, we do have to fundamentally think the same about one thing: we have to agree that there is value in every person.

The first step to this agreement is noting that there is a stark difference between looking *at* someone and looking *up* to someone, and then choosing the latter as our default. We have to stop treating interactions—from an informal first meeting to a formal collaboration—like sightseeing trips and instead start embracing them like prospects of something greater before us.

Not only opportunities for greater success but also for lessons and memories that last a lifetime.

Two years ago, I was using an airplane bathroom when a man pushed open the door while I was sitting on the toilet. I know. I couldn't reach the latch to lock it. I hate to say it, but this wasn't the first time. The man was horrified the nanosecond he saw me sitting there with my legs sticking straight out. He immediately yanked the door closed. It was quite a violent door slam. Apparently, he found another bathroom, because when I returned to my seat, he was already back in his. Conveniently, this was right across the aisle from me.

When I sat back down, I leaned his way and whispered, "Are you going to remember this day as long as I will?" He burst out laughing, and I joined in.

"I think so," he answered, with bright eyes.

When we landed about thirty minutes later, he leaned over to me and asked if he could help me retrieve my bags from the overhead bin.

"Yes," I said. "Thank you."

"It's the least I can do!" he replied with a big grin.

CHAPTER 7

ASKING FOR HELP IS A STRENGTH, NOT A WEAKNESS

Learning to depend on one another is a challenge in our current day and age. Independence is still the prized trait. It's commonly seen as a sign of physical capability, emotional strength, and even an innovative mind. While all these things might very well be true of an independent person, there's one common element of independence we never talk about, maybe because it ruins the anecdotal heroes we've lauded for so long. Independence has limits.

One day early in my career, my supervisor called me in and I didn't know why. He was a sharp systems guy in his midforties, short, with glasses, and slightly balding. His relational approach, which I appreciated, was direct. He didn't pull punches and said only what was needed. I sat on the very uncomfortable pleather chair opposite his desk, and he wasted no time explaining that my coworker who supported the other half of the company's sales reporting system was moving to a new job.

"You're going to take over his part of the system too," he instructed.

"I will support the whole system, end to end?"

"Yes, that's right."

This was the proving ground I'd sought. It was all up to me, and I felt confident I could do it. Then the first of July came, and my system began running its quarterly processes, which detailed when, where, and how much of our products sold around the world.

As you can probably imagine, the quarterly sales results were always eagerly anticipated by the sales and marketing folks. My phone would typically ring early and often when a quarterly report was due, to make sure it was coming. Meetings hinged on the reports. Bonuses were won and lost. People banked promotions on the numbers I was charged with providing. The hope around the office was that the numbers were really up, so I was poised to be the bearer of good news. But then there was a glitch in the system the morning I went to run the reports.

I spent four hours trying to figure it out, making several calls to outside technical people. No one knew what to do. Keep in mind, this was the mid-1990s. I wasn't just clicking a button and getting an error message. I was typing commands into the prompt on the screen—commands that had worked in the past. I understood the system forward and backward, so I thought. At 1:00 p.m., a VP called to say his report had not been delivered. "I'm working on it," I assured him, but I needed someone to assure me. The VP's voice was the straw that broke the camel's back. I stepped out of my office and commenced the walk of shame into my supervisor's office, which I had never done to that point. I showed him printouts of the error, the system documentation, and the names of the tech experts I'd spoken to. I was at a complete loss, I confessed, and needed his advice. He looked over my stack of papers. Pecked at his computer some. Then, still staring at his screen, he confessed he was at a loss too. My body felt like a furnace. I was letting everyone down—people who had put a lot of faith in me.

I left my supervisor's office and walked to the bathroom, slower than my normal slow, racking my brain about what to do. As I pushed through the bathroom door, I whispered, "God, please help me; please guide me."

I was walking back to my office when a shadow came up behind me and covered my own. I giggled. "You can't sneak up on me!" I said playfully and turned to see who it was. There wasn't a soul in sight. I stood statue still for a moment, swiveling only my eyes left and right. No one, and no sign of anyone either. For a minute I forgot my dilemma. Then something snapped me back into reality, and I hurried to my desk.

I looked at my screen and the same error message I'd been staring at all day. Suddenly, it came to me. I saw where the problem could be. I pecked at my keyboard for fifteen minutes. Then I ran a test report. No error message. It worked! I initiated the real reports this time, and they began populating.

I hurried down the hall to my supervisor's office to tell him the good news.

"How'd you fix it?" he asked.

"Divine intervention."

"No, really," he replied.

"I'm serious," I insisted.

He looked at me and could see that I wasn't joking.

"Whatever it takes," he concluded. "Nice work."

I never explained to him the whole story of what had happened in the hall outside the bathroom. I guess I had the sense that God wanted me to enjoy that win. And maybe he also wanted me to see that I couldn't do it alone. It was a lesson I've never forgotten.

In truth, that inexplicable story did more than remind me that I needed help; it was a stronger reminder that I shouldn't be afraid to ask for help.

A company in the construction industry of the 1990s, Caterpillar was a male-dominated workplace. The IT department where I initially worked was no exception. My male coworkers treated me fairly, but I was still an outlier in more ways than one. My first supervisor was a strong woman named Diane who walked with a slight limp from childhood polio. She became my first work mentor. Diane told me the truth, and she was never shy about giving me the toughest assignments so that I could prove myself. She believed in me, and I know her faith had something to do with the fact that she could see herself in me. Years later, when I was a more seasoned employee and working in management myself, she and I looked back together, and she told me she was pulling for me from day one. She said she could see I had the skills to do well at Caterpillar, but she hoped I also had the drive and humility to match it.

Neither timing nor some stroke of luck is responsible for Caterpillar becoming the nearly $55 billion behemoth it is today. In my thirty years there, I can honestly say that the leadership was always innovative and open-minded, meaning the leaders were, like Diane, never afraid to believe in what others could do, no matter who they were. Everyone from every department in every position was valuable. That was the assumption from the outset. You still had to prove that assumption correct. You couldn't get lazy with the belief that had been placed in you.

I was grateful Diane had given me the springboard to continually make good on my employer's bet on me. I don't know how I would have fared if my first foray into corporate America had been overshadowed by prejudice. I was young and inexperienced, and though I felt I had the raw skill set to succeed, I still needed the opportunities to hone those skills even more.

To give another person an opportunity to affirm his or her value can sometimes be seen in the wrong light. We might be tempted to think that having to "prove" ourselves shouldn't be necessary if someone truly believes in us. I think that's the incorrect take, especially in a collaborative environment. Even if a group effort is launched on the assumption of mutual value, how that effort plays out, and whether it is successful or not, has everything to do with what each person does with his or her preassigned badge of value. This doesn't mean that if I let another person down, I no longer have value. It means the value others assign me should be stewarded well. It is right that it's given to us, as it's right for us to assume value in others. But we should never take lightly the value assigned to us.

At Caterpillar, I wanted to show my bosses and coworkers that I belonged not only as a teammate but also as a person who was worthy of their trust. My inclination was to let my work speak for itself and to get the job done, no questions asked. But this inclination battled against a higher principle: that asking for help was a strength, not a weakness. The trouble was that in my new environment, asking for help was not necessarily seen as a strength. Unfortunately, it rarely is.

In places such as shops and supermarkets, asking someone to reach a can of beans for me or grab a shirt off the rack rarely rubs people the wrong way, particularly in places where employees are paid to serve the customer. However, in a corporate environment, there are often unspoken rules about being the "squeaky wheel" or the "weak link." Inside the muscular walls of Caterpillar, everyone worked to repel those labels. And trust me: I didn't want anyone to think those things of me either. I also knew I'd need help more often than most, even if it was to reach a file folder from the supply closet. I hoped my work overpowered any notion that I was a weak link. ·

"Whatever it takes" was a more fitting response than my IT boss realized that day I almost laid a big, fat egg. Sometimes success takes being the giver. Sometimes success takes being the receiver. We live in a world where the givers get the accolades. I ran a foundation, so obviously I'm grateful for the generosity of others. But I've learned that while it might feel better to give than to receive, it takes more strength to ask for help than to give it. This is especially the case in the working world, where we are expected to own our work and not disrupt others from theirs. I certainly understand the spirit behind the expectation, but it often goes too far and prohibits us from achieving our highest effectiveness together.

The truth is, I could not get through a day of my life without asking for help. A sampling of objects I cannot reach: elevator buttons for high floors, the overhead compartment on airplanes, the latch in airplane bathrooms (as you know), groceries above the second shelf, dead bolts, anything you set on my car roof, or under the windshield wipers, or on my car hood. When I rejected living on the fringe of society, I chose to spend my life with a constant level of reliance on others. It might sound like that makes me needy. It's the opposite. The biggest life we can live is not an independent one—it's an interdependent one.

In an article for *Psychology Today*, longtime clinical and forensic psychologist Dr. Michael Karson explained, "The relational posture we call independence is not, after all, independent of other people but is instead one that requires the 'independent' person to avoid appearing needy, and since we are an extremely socially needy animal, maintaining that appearance can wear you down."[1]

He goes on to explain that the act of remaining independent keeps us from important interdependent gestures, like asking friends if we talked too much at a meal or expressing hurt feelings over something someone else did or said. The deeper and more significant our relationship with another person, the more damage independence can do. I think we all know what happens when one person in a relationship feels he or she is unnecessary. Suddenly, what

The biggest life we can live is not an independent one—it's an interdependent one.

began under the banner of partnership or collaboration or unity becomes divided into what you do and say and what I do and say. There is no "we" or "us" except maybe in physical proximity.

If I'm a very independent leader in a corporate setting, I might be around my team all day long. I might even spend more time around the people I'm charged to lead than I do by myself. However, if I never express my feelings, never ask for help, and never ask those around me for feedback on how I'm doing as a leader . . . how I can do better . . . where I've already gone wrong . . . then I'm not a member of the team. I'm just a figurehead. The others might work well together and be truly interdependent on one another, but my actions reveal that I operate independent of them.

I realize how this might make you feel if you're someone who built success on being independent. What I can tell you from my own experience is that in most settings there's a fine line between independence and interdependence. The way you can usually tell which side you're on is your personal and corporate growth. Independence has a ceiling. Without others, you will only grow so much as an individual. Has your personal growth stalled in recent years? Without others, your efforts will only climb so high. Has your latest venture plateaued?

This isn't to say you can't go very far independently. There's no doubt you can. But eventually, every solo artist is faced with a critical question: Which is more important, continued growth or continued independence?

This was a question I had to ask myself often as a young teenager. Like most people that age, I'd been dreaming of more independence. I wanted that storied chance to express my own ideas and take my own actions, without having to ask for opinions or permission. Michele's version of *To Kill a Mockingbird*; *Little Women*; *The Lion, the Witch and the Wardrobe*; and *A Tree Grows in Brooklyn*, all in one. My parents were good about giving my siblings and me test runs in this department as we grew older. They were more aggressive with me, though, probably because they felt the need to fight back any tendency I might have had to embrace shyness and indifference. They'd learned enough about little people to know that a quiet life at home was the easier path for someone in my shoes, but not necessarily the best path. Honestly, letting me create a safe world at home would have been easier for them too. I'm fortunate they didn't take the easy road.

The older I got, the more I realized that their leadership in my life wasn't just for me. They were constantly looking for people to lift up. I saw this most regularly in their involvement with the Little People of America (LPA). If you recall, it was my mom who had originally come across an article in *Reader's Digest* about LPA and written them on my behalf. It was through LPA that I met a whole roomful of little people for the first time. This wasn't a onetime event. That day at JoAnne's house in Springfield was the beginning of a lifetime of involvement with a community that has mastered the art of interdependence.

The LPA isn't like a typical organization. To join isn't about a social badge of honor. You don't get reduced green fees, cheaper hotel rates, or car rental reward points. What you get is access to thousands of people who understand that navigating life together is better than navigating it solo. The

LPA is ultimately about listening; sharing resources, tips, and recommendations; and always looking for opportunities to serve one another, all in the common pursuit of living a full and fulfilling life as a little person. A unique trait of the LPA is that it is nearly always a family affair. All family members benefit. The parents of little people usually join on behalf of their children when they are young, in the hopes that LPA will (1) help their children see their full potential and (2) help the parents support their children in this quest. The dynamic gives the LPA gatherings an instant air of camaraderie. While there's certainly some letting our hair down—and occasionally too down—at some of the get-togethers, the overarching spirit is devotion to one another.

Now, I should say here that many parents who join don't know this is the case from day one. A good bit of them are joining LPA out of a mix of confusion and curiosity, and the hope I mentioned above. They hear about LPA or read about it like my mom did and they think something like, *Well, that couldn't hurt.* Or at times they're looking for some certainty in circumstances that feel very uncertain. This was particularly the case in the 1970s, when my parents and I joined. Resources for little people were nonexistent. A physician like Dr. Kopits was an anomaly. To meet someone of his stature who had dedicated his work to helping people of my stature was like my family winning the lottery. And it wouldn't have happened if not for the LPA. My parents never forgot this connection, and at every LPA event they looked for opportunities to lift up others by telling them about Dr. Kopits or offering a parenting recommendation. The more they learned, the more they wanted to help. As a result, they never stopped learning. Despite their inner strength, they never stopped seeking help. As I got older, I began to see that this approach wasn't just about them and me. They viewed help from others as a treasured resource they could pay forward. When they were helped, they were being given something they could turn around and share.

. . .

Twenty-three years ago, Terry and Billie gave birth to a daughter with dwarfism. She was their firstborn, and Billie was twenty-eight when she had her. They named her Ciara, and when she was three, they attended their first local LPA event, which was being held at a downtown Peoria hotel. I was thirty and nearly a decade into my career at CAT by this time. My parents were in their fifties. But we were still there. (My mom and I still attend to this day.) When Terry, Billie, and Ciara walked through the double doors and into the room where the first night's dinner and dance were being held, there must have been a certain look about them that told my parents it was their first time. Mom and Dad waved them over to our table. I was already mingling with others at this point.

When they sat down, my dad asked if this was their first LPA meeting. They said yes. They then introduced themselves and exchanged a minute of small talk. My dad then asked what type of dwarfism Ciara had.

"She has achondroplasia," Billie replied.

"That's the most common kind!" my mom chimed in.

Terry's and Billie's faces softened. Smiles rose naturally. For the next thirty minutes, my parents and Ciara's shared stories. Theirs were fresh, like wounds still healing. They'd brought a lot of uncertainty to the event that night. They'd also brought hope. My parents elevated the couple's hope above their uncertainties. They told Terry and Billie about me as a little girl, my first difficult day of kindergarten, my many surgeries, and the comical nature of getting me back and forth from Baltimore. They also shared their own fears and challenges, opened their storehouse of resources, and even sent another young couple to their house to show them household items they might want to update, things like lower light switches and levered door handles instead of round ones. Still, the sum of my parents' message was clear: "Treat her like you would any other child. She's going to be just fine."

Terry and Billie took it all in and asked every question that had been swirling in their heads. By the time I returned to the table, the four of them were laughing and my dad was bouncing Ciara on his lap. They already knew me pretty well, and the ensuing friendship was easy. Billie and Terry were my peers, after all. Ciara was a beautiful light in our world. In her I could see my young self. Happy, innocent, and unaware of the challenges that lay ahead—not just the physical ones but the emotional ones too. Right there I decided I was going to be for Ciara what so many had been for me. I would be her biggest fan and advocate, and I would open doors for her. As far as I could help it, she would never believe she was not enough, not loved, not capable.

As Ciara grew, Billie and I kept in close touch. They lived in St. Louis, and whenever I was down that way, I'd call her up and go visit. I'd also invite them to come up anytime I had a pool party. As a little girl, Ciara loved to swim. So did her younger sister, born three years after Ciara, without dwarfism. Every time I met a little person Ciara's age over the years, I'd call Billie and introduce her to the other mom. By the time Ciara was having her surgeries, the medical procedures had advanced a lot, and her recovery didn't require the same lengthy hospital stay that mine did. I wanted to make sure Ciara had friends who understood her condition, like the friends I'd had at Children's Hospital those five teenage summers. I wanted her to experience the camaraderie I did so that her self-esteem would never suffer. Today, Ciara is twenty-seven and happily married.

I remember a few years after that first meeting, when Terry, Billie, and Ciara were sitting with my parents at another LPA event and a young couple in their midtwenties walked through the door, a little girl with dwarfism being carried in the mom's arms. Terry looked over at my parents, expecting them to invite the young couple over to our table.

My mom shook her head. "No, no," she said with a smile. "It's now your turn to pay it forward."

Billie nodded and grinned. She then stood up and walked over to invite the new family to our table. And the string has continued every year since.

This was and still is the tribal nature of the LPA. To this day, if I have a question about anything—from an issue at school, to adapting a kitchen, extensions for a car, or dating—I can dial up any one of thousands of LPA members. You know what I'll hear on the other end? Without fail, no matter what time of day or season of life, when I say I need help with something, the response will be immediate. I'll hear, "Tell me what

I can do," or "I'll be right there." I'll hear, "You can use mine," or "Go here, and tell them I sent you." And sometimes, when it's what is needed most, I'll hear nothing but the sniffles and tears that match my own.

Can you imagine if we were all part of a tribe like this? It's possible—but only if we can accept that we all need help from one another from time to time.

When I took over the leadership of the Caterpillar Foundation in 2011, I wanted to bring this same philosophy to the work we did. I was once asked by the *Atlantic* how we manage to collaborate with such a wide array of other organizations—from Feeding America and the Nature Conservancy to the American Red Cross and Water.org—and my initial answer was that we have to if we want to accomplish big initiatives. How we work together is another story. To spur legitimate entrepreneurial opportunities in impoverished countries or supply clean water in desolate climates, it takes more than one person with a big checkbook or a big idea. Part of the criteria we established for selecting any partner charity is its willingness and ability to foster additional alliances with other nonprofits as well as private ventures and government organizations. This is what I call the three-legged stool because when multiple parties are brought into the philosophy of sharing resources, the parties are also brought into the philosophy that acknowledging our need for one another is what upholds us. I've had the privilege of seeing this powerful dynamic play out many times through my work with the Caterpillar Foundation.

On a beautiful day a few hours outside of Kigali, Rwanda, I was once again visiting with a co-op of farmers. As the van pulled up to a very large parcel of land at ten in the morning, I could see several tents already set up. About 250 people, Rwandan farmers mostly, were seated under and around the tents. Just beyond them, I could see that the parcel of land was full of beautiful, healthy crops. I stepped out of the van, and the co-op's leader and a local official welcomed me. As I made my way to my seat, everyone was surprised to see me, but they smiled big nonetheless. I sat right in the middle of them. The co-op leader then introduced me to John (not knowing I'd met him on my first trip to Uganda), an agriculture specialist from Opportunity International (OI). John had been faithfully educating farmers in the area on best practices for growing crops for many years. This latest group of farmers had also received small loans to fund their farms.

As their tradition goes, before anyone else spoke, a group of local women glowing in bright-colored dresses stepped to the front and performed a mesmerizing dance. The soft skin on their arms and faces glistened in the hot sun as their dresses ebbed and flowed like ocean waves against a vivid sunset. I have always loved when people take such pride in their culture. No matter where I am, it moves me to watch something like their dance.

When the women in the bright dresses were finished, we all clapped. Immediately, several women—even some from the group of dancers—lined up at the mic. The first woman to speak was in her thirties and wore a bright orange–and–black dress. She was clearly nervous, so I smiled at her and leaned forward to show her I was very interested in what she had to say. She looked right at me and said, "My name is Keza." She then explained that her husband had left her and her children a few years ago. Tears welled in her eyes, and she looked down and started to fidget with her dress. She took a breath and resumed, still casting her glance low.

"It was up to me to support my family," she said softly in a lovely Rwandan accent. "But, I needed help."

She explained that through another person there in the audience, she had been introduced to a loan officer at OI to ask about getting a small loan to plant crops there on the field behind her. She glanced over her shoulder. When her eyes returned to the crowd, she again looked right at me.

"I could not do it on my own," she confessed, explaining that the first year the crops were not great, but she'd scraped up enough money to keep her family fed.

"Then," she continued, "other farmers in the co-op and John taught me how to plant and take care of the crops to get the best yield. I took all the help I could get. And my yields began to increase." As she spoke, her chin lifted and her shoulders aligned with confidence. I could see the pride she had in those crops. "Michele," she then said, with her voice now at full crescendo, "last year I was able to buy a house for my family. My children are in school, and my family has a home and a future." Her face broke into a huge smile. "I couldn't have done all of this without the help of many people." She bowed her head in gratitude.

I can rarely hold back my tears, and I failed to once again. I looked at her and wiped away the tears.

"I can't tell you how proud I am to know you, Keza," I said. "So many people were pulling for you." I reminded her how brave she was. I explained to her that accepting the help of others showed her strength and her passion to take care of her family. I also reminded her that what she wants, most mothers want—to provide for their families.

"You were a big part in your success as well," I concluded.

When she finished, Keza walked to my seat and handed me two large ears of maize. I'm not kidding—the cobs were thicker and longer than one of my arms. What a crop! It was such a priceless gift to me because those gorgeous cobs were tangible pictures of the results of healthy interdependence.

When we grow from children to adults, the expectation is that we begin to take on more and more responsibility for our behavior and choices until we eventually take full responsibility. I think we see this in the wrong light as adults. We translate full responsibility to mean that we can't ask for help because asking for help indicates we aren't taking responsibility. This is pretty ludicrous if you think about it.

I can take full responsibility for my behavior and choices and still recognize there are resources I don't have that are required if I'm going to go as far as I am compelled to go. I'd even say that taking full responsibility *requires* fully recognizing what resources you have and what resources you don't.

We get heroism wrong when we paint a picture of someone who overcomes every challenge and reaches the pinnacle of potential solo, in a vacuum, with only his or her own resources. Yes, redemption is one of the most beautiful stories on the planet. When a person who wasn't supposed to succeed does anyway, we celebrate him. When a person is dealt a bad hand and adversity is forced on her, and she becomes great in spite of it, we rejoice. And in both cases, we should. But we have to peel back the layers of those stories to see that neither the fighter nor the overcomer ever does it alone. And we have to be willing to acknowledge that a hero having help doesn't detract from the beauty and inspiration of what he or she has done.

For those of us living in America, independence is part of our country's brand. Every Fourth of July, we celebrate it. Our nation's history carries stories of individuals who stood for what they believed in, resisted challengers, and won the day on the back of their own resources. At least that's how we characterize them in many books and movies. The reality we can miss in the story of America is that we didn't seek independence from one another; we sought a new, united opportunity to thrive together. Seen in that light, independence is something worth fighting for. But it's not mutually exclusive of interdependence. That's where we get off track as adults.

The mental health community used to view dependence as a weakness. In the last decade this view has changed. Now these professionals see dependence as a trait everyone shares. The real issue is no longer *whether* someone is dependent on others. The issue is now *to what degree* is someone dependent on others. In everyday terms, we're all on the spectrum of dependence, with unhealthy outcomes at both the overly dependent end and the overly independent end. The healthiest people among us are those who balance a reliance on the help of others with an ability to work independently.

"Interdependence is both a fact of life and an orientation to life," wrote Dr. Miki Kashtan, cofounder of Bay Area Nonviolent Communication and consultant at the Center for Efficient Collaboration. "Whether or not we consciously engage with the interdependence of life it continues to happen. . . . Whether we like it or not, whether we know about it or not, all things are interdependent."[2]

When I was a newborn baby in my parents' home, I was helpless. So were you. We were completely dependent on our moms and dads or other caregivers to keep us alive. As we got older, we were given more responsibility and taught that we could depend on ourselves to get important tasks done. When we became adults, most of us felt the immediate pressure to become completely independent, whether directly through our parents' actions or indirectly through cultural expectations. But is the goal of adulthood to be wholly self-sufficient? Haven't we seen that staunch self-sufficiency in adulthood leads to as many problems as helpless dependence in adulthood?

I remember when I heard about the 1993 suicide of Hervé Villechaize, the actor who played Tattoo on *Fantasy Island*. I'd only met him once, but his death felt personal anyway. Though I didn't know all the details, I was saddened and felt compassion for him as I would for anyone who gets to that point. Then, in 2018, filmmaker Sacha Gervasi made an HBO film about his conversations with Villechaize days before the actor's death. In an article for *Vanity Fair*, Julie Miller explored the film, titled *My Dinner with Hervé*, and Gervasi's understanding of what brought Villechaize to the point of taking his own life.

His father had been a doctor in Paris when Villechaize was born in 1943, she explained. When he learned that his son had dwarfism, he took Hervé to medical clinics in three different countries in hopes of curing him. "At a young age," explained Miller, "Villechaize was subjected to barbaric treatments. . . . He did not grow taller than three foot ten; Villechaize was bullied mercilessly." According to his brother, he was kicked in the head while walking down the street just for being different.[3]

Villechaize managed to overcome the abuse and, at eighteen, became the youngest artist to be shown in the Museum of Paris. He had immense talent. Then his father insisted he go to New York to pursue theater, telling him, "Go where the freaks go. Go to New York."[4] Villechaize complied, and in Greenwich Village his acting career was born. It ended abruptly in 1983 when he was fired for requesting to be paid equal to his costar, Ricardo Montalbán. His acting career was effectively over after that. He appeared in a handful of commercials over the next decade, but no one seemed to want his services any longer. Villechaize retreated into obscurity as he struggled with legal and financial trouble and increasing health issues. He began to drink too much. On many nights, he poured two bottles of wine into his ninety-pound body. The isolation. Being unseen and overlooked. It was coming to a head. In the weeks before his death, two Houston radio deejays were heard mercilessly mocking Villechaize over the air. On September 5, 1993, when he took his own life, he left a note. Among his final words were these: "At 6 years old I knew there was no place for me . . . Never one knew my pain—for 40 years—or more." He singled out his three brothers for never caring anything about him, citing an incident that had occurred in 1955, when he would have been about twelve.[5]

When actor Billy Barty formed the LPA in 1957, he did so not only to dignify the lives of little people like himself and Hervé Villechaize—a fourteen-year-old budding artist then—he also wanted to create a place where little people could ask for and find the help they needed in a world that so often overlooked them. Unfortunately, one of the harsh realities of today's world is that so many of us who need help don't get it for one reason or another. Sometimes we're afraid to ask. Sometimes being asked feels like a burden. *Help* is not a four-letter word. It defines our existence.

Thirteen years after I was born, my mother was going about her business at home when the phone rang. This was the year after she'd discovered the LPA in a *Reader's Digest* and found Dr. Kopits. My mom picked up the phone, and on the other end of the line was Dr. Roark, the man who'd delivered me and told my parents, "Take her home and treat her like everybody else." My mom was immediately curious as to why he was calling; she knew he'd retired several years earlier. She didn't realize this call wasn't about me.

Dr. Roark was straightforward. He told my mom that his child had just given birth to a baby with achondroplasia. Since he'd been a general practitioner, neither he nor his family knew a specialist on dwarfism. He wanted to know if my parents had learned anything about dwarfism since my birth, and if they would be willing to share that information. My mom told him what she'd learned, which at that point was largely about the LPA and Dr. Kopits. She then reminded him of the profound advice he'd given my parents on the day I was born.

It wasn't a long conversation and we never heard from him again, but I've always appreciated that small detail in my story because it's a great reminder of how important asking for help is. Once again crossing paths with Dr. Roark was also

Despite all the attention we give to individualism, one of life's most powerful realities is that we thrive because of others, not in spite of them.

a reminder that people are brought into our lives for a reason—even if that reason isn't revealed until many years after the initial encounter. When I was born, little was known about dwarfism in the medical field. My parents still asked for help and even in his lack of knowledge, Dr. Roark had helped them through his profound words that changed the course of my life. When his grandchild was born, Dr. Roark was the one asking for help. He asked my mom and even in her lack of knowledge, she offered the only recommendations she had at the time. We heard through the grapevine that the baby had been taken to see Dr. Kopits. When we learned this, we knew they were going to be fine.

Despite all the attention we give to individualism, one of life's most powerful realities is that we thrive because of others, not in spite of them. It's easy to forget, but this reality never changes as you grow from newborn to adult. The sooner we collectively grasp this, the sooner we access the full scope of resources all around us. And the sooner we see the treasure we possess that can be given to others.

CHAPTER 8

CHOOSE INTIMACY
OVER INFLUENCE

L asting impact rarely happens from a distance, in the peripheral. By the time I entered the workforce, I had met dozens of disabled and disadvantaged people whose lives were being lived out along the periphery of society, out of harm's way, often resulting in isolation and depression. I knew what I was risking by walking into the center of the corporate fray. I knew I'd be hurt, on accident and on purpose. I'd be knocked down, physically and emotionally. I also understood that the middle of the action is the only place where we can make the biggest impact on one another's lives.

Growing up, school became a safe place once the kids got to know me for being smart instead of being small. The world outside school remained a less friendly, less interested world. It was there I had to learn to balance taking initiative with asking for help. The question was, how? At my size, the opportunities to learn were few and far between because most who didn't already know me opted to skirt an introduction, never mind a relationship. This treatment didn't change, by and large, until I began working at CAT, where I was around the same people day after day.

When a rare job became available—internally it was called an "interdepartmental liaison"—in what was the cat's meow division of the company, called the North American Commercial Division, I felt I was a perfect fit. Now nearly a decade into my career, I believed I had proven my value to the company in multiple roles and departments. However, I didn't yet know protocol for requesting consideration for a new position. Fortunately, I didn't have to. A supervisor in the division, named Alice, knew my skills and offered me the position. I was thrilled. But when I walked in on my first day, I was instantly met by familiar feelings of inadequacy.

As I navigated the halls to my new office, I walked by the windows of my coworkers, all of them clean-shaven, all-American, white males. All they could see was the top of my head. I could hear the shuffling of feet and squeaking of chair springs as they craned their necks to see who belonged to the mysterious head bobbing down the hall. It was like kindergarten all over again. But this time I was older and knew better.

Instead of putting my head down and focusing on building credibility invisibly, I took a step further and focused on meeting my coworkers' needs, perhaps ones they didn't even know they had. As an IT person, I was always in a supportive role whenever someone needed me. In my new position, I tried to place myself in their roles from the get-go instead of performing my way to their respect.

I carved out time each week to get creative about providing better solutions than they currently had. I also made time to ask my coworkers directly, "What else can I do that would make life easier for you?" It was an upgrade—a very important upgrade—in my career, from a focus on excellence to a focus on service excellence.

Three months into my new position, a walk down that same hallway triggered a different response. "Michele! Come in, come in!" and "I just wanted to say thanks!" were common refrains. For a time, I couldn't make it to my office without someone calling me into his.

The establishment of my camaraderie with these men was significant timing. One October day, I was with my dad when he died suddenly of a heart attack. He had always been my rock, my model of strength, and the one man who stood taller than every other in my life. There was suddenly a hole in my universe, and I knew it would never be filled. But the loss lit a fire under me to make the biggest impact I could with my life. I knew I would carry on his legacy. If I could, I would take it even further.

When the Six Sigma Master Black Belt position opened up at CAT shortly thereafter, I knew it was an ideal opportunity to expand my impact within the company. Six Sigma is a strategy for corporate process improvement that was created in the 1980s by a Motorola engineer named Bill Smith. When Jack Welch made the approach integral to General Electric's business strategy in the 1990s, the popularity of Six Sigma exploded, and numerous companies began ushering their employees into the certification process, from yellow belt to green belt to black belt and, finally, master black belt. The master black belt's job is to act as a liaison between the organization's improvement programs, the company's current black belts, and the executive leadership. Essentially, the leadership position is responsible for collaborating to ensure growth and process excellence within the entire organization, from top to bottom. For the first time in my career, I went to my department head and advocated for myself, telling him I felt I was a fit for the job. I don't think I would've been so bold had my dad's legacy not compelled me.

My boss later recounted to me that when he brought my name into the meeting, the business unit leadership agreed unanimously that I could take the position to the next level. I got the job and was given enormous responsibility.

There were two ironies with my promotion. One, the smallest woman in the company now played the role of key collaborator in the business unit. It made me giggle when I thought of it. Two, the one person in the company who relied most on her coworkers' support had become her coworkers' primary advocate. Ultimately, the new position was a clear illustration that impact is about more than stature. (I loved telling people outside of CAT that I was a master black belt. The reactions were priceless.) I was in the prime position to help others, but I would always need help to carry out my job too. I became a walking, rolling billboard for corporate interdependence. The effect seemed to take hold immediately.

When I moved to my new building, the facilities manager gave me fits again—this time about designating a parking spot for me at a different building. However, someone had my back without me asking. When Bill, the marketing vice president, saw I was parking in the drop-off circle every day, he called the facilities manager into his office and, in no uncertain terms, told him he had one week to create a parking spot for me and one day to give him the plan for how he was going to do it. Three days later, I had a private parking garage in the loading docks, with a key fob opener to boot!

Though they probably never knew it, when coworkers like Bill stood up for me in ways I couldn't, in ways that my father who knew me well would have, it was among the greatest gifts I ever received at Caterpillar. Every time it happened, I was reminded of the same thing—that influence is intimate.

One of my first major leadership roles was taking over the parts authorizations division of Caterpillar. My team's main responsibility was to determine the proper placement of CAT parts to ensure continued availability and an ongoing presence throughout the world. I had five supervisors on my team to help me manage this major responsibility. One of them was Rose, an attractive, five-foot-eleven, blond woman who was known to handle herself well. She was stationed in Panama, so I only had one occasion to meet her, at our division's annual holiday party. We spoke for five minutes and decided I would come visit her and her team in a few months. The time came that winter, and I boarded a plane for the Tocumen International Airport in Panama City. I was prepared for a work trip. I didn't know it would be much more.

Rose picked me up on a Friday night and drove me through downtown Panama City to my hotel. She pointed out colonial-era landmarks and the flower-filled plazas along the way. I was struck by the way the city's lights shimmered off the Pacific Ocean. When she dropped me at my hotel, we agreed she'd pick me up the following morning, early enough that I'd have a chance to introduce myself to the team members before we sat down to meet.

Following our team meeting the next morning, Rose and I had lunch at my hotel. As we wrapped up, we discussed plans to reconvene that evening for dinner at a restaurant that highlighted the wonderful Panamanian food and culture. We'd have enough time afterward to enjoy ourselves a little more before I had to return to the States. She dropped me back at my hotel, where I intended to rest and freshen up before she returned.

Once in my room, I replayed our lunch conversation. We'd discussed her assignment, which was to hire and train a team for a big project there. I'd shared with Rose that I wanted to learn more about how the team was structured to ensure it was optimized. It had caused some awkward tension because here was the boss, asking questions about an assignment the boss herself had just joined. Rose had been in Panama three months, and I was new on the scene. I was rethinking my approach when the phone in my room rang.

The man on the other end said he was Frank, an employee whom I'd met at the morning meeting. His cadence was quick. "Something has happened at Rose's apartment," he said, "and you need to come right away."

My heart dropped. I asked for the basic details and then said, "I'll be there as fast as I can." I hung up and left my room right away, and as I was walking down the hall, another door opened; it was the company psychologist from headquarters. Unbeknownst to me, he was there to visit the facility too.

"John, come with me," I said as I hurried forward. "We have a situation." I explained what I knew.

"Where does she live?" John asked.

I realized I had no idea. Then I remembered being on the main street along the water the night before, and Rose saying, "That white building with a blue fish is my building."

We asked the front desk for a car, and as soon as we jumped in, I said in broken Spanish, *"Blanco hotel con peces, al derecho, por favor."*

The driver stared blankly at me in the rearview mirror. I repeated the same thing, emphasizing *"al derecho,"* or "to the right," so he'd at least get going in the right direction. I knew he would have to drive down the main drag that way, and I hoped I'd remember the building when I saw it. I told John that all I knew from the drive the night before was that Rose's apartment building was white with a blue fish on it. John and I then discussed the best way to approach the situation.

"Let her do most of the talking," John advised. "If she wants to. Just be present for her."

There were at least ten police cruisers parked in front of the apartment building. We jumped out of the car and followed the police into the elevator. When the doors opened, I looked to the left, and there were two closed apartment doors. Then I looked to the right, and the door closest to me had been bashed in, and the doorframe was hanging down. Frank appeared in the doorway.

"Where is she?" I said.

"The back bedroom," Frank replied.

I told John I would go back by myself, not knowing what condition Rose was in. I carefully navigated through her belongings that were scattered all over the floor. Rose was sitting on the bed, with her head in her hands. I sat next to her and placed my arm on her back. I said nothing. Finally, she spoke up and explained what had happened.

She'd returned to her apartment after our lunch to find the door smashed in. She stepped inside and quickly realized that her home had been burglarized. She immediately returned to the hallway and called the elevator, planning to go back to the lobby to find help. When the elevator doors opened, three men with handfuls of her belongings were standing there. A scuffle ensued, and she was punched in the chest and shoved to the floor. She got up and the scuffle spilled back into her apartment, where she stood her ground and eventually scared them off. She had been roughed up but, thankfully, wasn't seriously injured, at least not physically. She was still rattled emotionally.

After she finished, I reassured her and said little more than, "We will do whatever you need." I then asked John to come in and speak to Rose separately. He was a professional, and I knew he could help in a way I couldn't.

After John spent a few minutes with Rose, I took her back to my hotel, where I got her a room across the hall from me. I told her she could be alone or stay with me that night, or we could sit up and talk. I then offered to call her parents. She was a single twenty-seven-year-old at the time, so her parents were the first call. It was hard for them to hear what had happened, but I tried my best to set them at ease and let them know we were going to take care of their daughter. Rose's job responsibilities, missing time at work, continuing the project . . . these details never once crossed my mind given the gravity of what had happened. But as the evening wound down, she told me she didn't know if she wanted to stay in Panama.

"Take some time off, Rose," I said. "Think through what you want to do."

I reassured her that no matter what she decided, I would support her. I knew that if she decided to step down from the project, I'd be in a major pickle. But I didn't care. The next day she flew back to San Diego to be with her parents. I told her I'd call in a week to see what she wanted to do. When I called, she said she was ready to return to Panama. She wanted to see the commitment she'd made to the team and the company through.

"I'll come back with you," I told her.

Two days later, she and I met in the Atlanta airport en route to Panama. I decided to stay with Rose that first week back to make sure she landed on her feet. She was so impressive. I knew the trauma was still with her, but her honesty and courage to remain committed to her team was an inspiration. I wouldn't have thought any less of her if she'd opted out of the project. I'd have understood. But I was moved watching someone so strong leading others despite herself.

. . .

When I was in grade school, I would get knocked down in the hallways a lot. Kids would be running from one classroom to the next, and they would plow right over me. One particular day, my class was heading to recess. An older boy pummeled me from behind and I landed square on my forehead. I lay there flat on my stomach and face. I couldn't move. I heard my teacher running over. She picked me up and hurried me to the front office. I could tell what was going on, but it was fuzzy, like a dream, and I couldn't keep my eyes open. I could hear everything, but I couldn't will my eyes to stay open. I was extremely nauseated. The school nurse called my mom and dad, and the minute they arrived, they rushed me to the ER. I was throwing up constantly by this point.

While I was on the gurney in the hospital, my parents kept repeating, "Michele, you have to keep your eyes open." I couldn't. I could not open my eyes. I remember the nurses insisting to my mom, "You have to get her to open her eyes and keep them open." This continued for three hours, with someone prying my eyelids open every few minutes, until I could finally open my eyes on my own. Everything was foggy and blurry, like an out-of-focus movie. We went home, and all through the night, my mom and dad took turns waking me up every hour. I'd sit up, throw up, and then go back to sleep. I missed a few days of school, but I finally returned to normal.

I remember dinner in our kitchen the evening of my first day back. My parents had obviously been storing up their advice until they knew I was fully cognizant.

"You know, Michele," said my mom, "you're not as big as everybody, and you're not going to be as big as everybody, so you have to be careful."

"They just bowl me over," I retorted.

"You can't be in the middle of everything, babe," my dad added. "You're exposed in every direction. You'll keep getting knocked down."

I trusted them and took their advice. From that day on, I walked down the sides of my school hallways to avoid the danger. But when I got older, I saw that I had to give up this strategy if I was going to make a difference in others' lives.

When I was a freshman in college at Bradley, where my mom worked, I had three jobs and a full course load, so I didn't have time to mill around. I had to get where I needed to go every day. During the second semester, I had to grab a quick lunch, and the student center was closest. I parked my car in a spot near the doors, but as I stepped from my car, I saw that a big ol' semi was parked at the curb right in front of the doors. Lest you think I'm merely lazy, you should know that walking around semitrucks for a little person is like walking around the block for an average-size person. The driver's door was facing the student center, so I couldn't ask him to move forward a little. I didn't have time for the roundabout journey, so I sized up the height of the truck's underside and thought it looked tall enough for me to walk right underneath. I nodded resolutely and went for it.

I got about halfway through and the engine started, lurching the semi forward a few inches. I'd like to tell you I said, "Oh, shoot," but that's not precisely what I said. The main issue was that I only have two speeds: sloth and turtle. In this case, for the first time in my life, I found a third speed: double-turtle. I wasn't exactly the little version of Usain Bolt, but you get my point. I wasn't near the tires, and the semi didn't start rolling until I was on the other side.

As I emerged from under the truck, I looked up at the driver's door. He was hanging his head and shoulder out the window and shaking his head. I waved at him and said, "Thanks for the shortcut." He laughed and gave me a thumbs-up. While I haven't walked under another semi since that day, I've always remembered the story because it pointed to an important relational lesson I was learning in my young adult life: the direct route is riskier, but it is often still the better route.

. . .

Rose and I bonded in Panama on that difficult day. It was a terrible circumstance that brought us together, but the circumstance broadened our understanding of the role that influence can and should play in our lives. It isn't based on hierarchy. It certainly isn't based on height. Influence is based on commitment to the other person, in spite of your differences, and regardless of the challenges involved in connecting and collaborating.

Rose and I have become very close since that 2007 incident in Panama. We've taken epic vacations together, sometimes just the two of us, and other times she has joined my family. We've shared long conversations about work and dreams and everything in between. Leadership has been a frequent topic.

Influence is based on commitment to the other person, in spite of your differences, and regardless of the challenges involved in connecting and collaborating.

She once admitted that before having me as her supervisor, she'd had mixed experiences with previous leaders. As a result, for her, the jury was out on me at the start—she was even a little skeptical.

I didn't know this at the time, of course, and I'm thankful I didn't, because I might have been tempted to take a self-serving approach. As it was, I did what I had learned to do in any collaborative role: I dug in and tried to learn as much about her as possible—her roles, her challenges, and her opportunities. How else could I be a good leader to her? It wasn't going to happen by assuming I knew anything. In fact, the only thing I assumed is that Rose knew herself better than I knew her, and that two heads were better than one and four hands better than two. (In meetings, I began to refer to our collaborative efforts as "the long and short of it.")

Rose is now in a leadership role herself, and one of her philosophies is that it is important to be personally invested in the people you work with and truly, deeply care about their lives and what impacts them. In Panama, she says the philosophy played out tangibly, first in how I led her through the trauma, and second in how she then led her team. She's concluded, as I have, that as leaders, it's critical to understand that your coworkers show up to work greatly affected by the things that happen outside of the office. Your job is to see them as real people, not just workers, with full lives, not just full-time jobs, that include many elements you probably know very little about. Sometimes work is the only stable part of a person's life. Sometimes going home is painful or frightening or lonely. A leader cannot ever overlook this.

The word *influence* has become a bit like old chewing gum. We've jawed about it for so long it has lost its original flavor. What does it mean these days? More important, what should it mean to those of us trying to make a lasting, positive impact in others' lives? People can manipulate and gain influence with others for their own purposes. Many do. People can lord their positions over people and hold influence over others. Many do. Are these both forms of influence? Technically, yes.

But they lack the catalytic element that allows influence to translate to impact. They lack intimacy.

When it comes to being a good leader, maybe we need to begin with a better word than *influence*. When we enter into a relationship with someone, if we're immediately thinking, *How can I influence this person?*, we're starting off with a huge assumption—that we know who that person is and what he or she needs. You can't lead from assumption if you want to have a lasting impact. You must lead from understanding, empathy, and compassion. When you understand what makes a person tick, what makes him sing and what drives him forward, you can walk alongside him and see the things he sees. The longer you walk with him, the more you're able to see things even he can't see and the more you're able to lead with vision for him.

I know I could have walked into Rose's apartment and done the professional thing and no one would have thought less of me. I could have made sure she was okay. I could have given her privacy and made sure the company covered the costs of flying her back home. I could have introduced her to a mental health professional so she could get the counsel she needed. All of these would have been well received. Instead, I sat down beside her, placed my hand on her shoulder, and didn't ask for answers. When she was ready, I made the call to her parents. Then I left the ultimate decision about what came next to her. I did all that based on what I knew of Rose, not simply upon a homogenized assumption that what was going on inside of her was what goes on inside all people who are traumatized by a violent robbery: she was unsettled; she was scared; she needed time to recover.

Is this generalized form of relating how we want to be

led? I think it hinders more than it helps. I'm so grateful I had leaders who chose to pursue intimacy before influence. They sought to learn before they tried to lead.

It's tempting as a leader to come into an organization or collaborative endeavor eager to make your mark and prove you can have an impact. What I've learned is that it's more important to first see, deeply, the people in the room. Only then can you have the vision to lead them well.

Sure, there is always risk in building your efforts at progress on real relationships with others. You'll be hurt. You might get yourself bowled over. But if you want to see lasting success, if you want to put a dent in the suffering in the world, if you want to truly elevate the lives of those around you, you can't do it from the sidelines. You have to enter into the relational fray. You have to get to know people.

Whenever I'm speaking from a stage, I like to hold up my size 1s and say, "It's impossible to walk in another person's shoes." It always gets a good laugh. Then I explain that while none of us can truly walk in another person's shoes, that doesn't mean we can't try

If you want to put a dent in the suffering in the world, if you want to truly elevate the lives of those around you, you can't do it from the sidelines.

and, in trying, understand in a more visceral way what it feels like to be that person. While we'll never quite understand the full scope of joy or pain in another's life, we should still seek to understand as much as we possibly can. There is great power in this comprehension. The more intimately acquainted you are with a person's life, her struggles and dreams, the easier it is to drop your self-serving slant.

The largest construction show in the Northern Hemisphere is called CONEXPO. Every three years, approximately 125,000 industry professionals gather at the Las Vegas Convention Center to preview the latest products and services being offered by more than 2,500 corporate exhibitors over nearly 3 million square feet of space. After I joined the Caterpillar Foundation, I saw CONEXPO as an opportunity to introduce hundreds of people to the work the foundation was doing around the world. We partnered with the organization known as "charity: water" to set up a "water walk" at Caterpillar's hospitality event one night. Down the middle of the five-thousand-square-foot ballroom, in stark contrast with the crystal chandeliers, buffets, open bar, and designer carpet, a seventy-five-foot path was lined with yellow five-gallon jugs of water.

Signage flanked the ballroom and exterior halls, bearing startling statistics:

- 663 million people do not have access to clean water
- 4,000 children die every day from waterborne disease
- African women, many of them young girls, spend 40 billion hours every year walking to fetch water that's the consistency and color of chocolate milk

Pictures of girls as young as eight, carrying the same five-gallon jugs, stood near the start of the walk.

The music faded as I was lifted onto a stage to explain what people were seeing. Each attendee could give someone access to clean water by picking up one or two jugs and walking the length of the path. For every walk completed, the Caterpillar

Foundation would donate to the charity to provide clean water on the individual's behalf. Every person who walked received a sticker on his or her shirt stating, "I Walked for Water."

As the evening continued, I could hear people asking others in the ballroom, "Did you do the walk?" Many walked more than once. One man walked one hundred times and wore his stickers proudly all over his shirt. A burly man wearing jeans, a polo, and a baseball hat walked up to me about halfway through the night. He must have just come upon the room because he asked me what was going on. "If you walk in a girl's shoes, we will donate to give someone clean water," I explained.

"What does carrying water have to do with girls?" he asked curiously.

"For families without access to water," I began, "it's usually the women or girls who walk hours every day to fetch water. The boys go to school; the girls fetch water instead of going to school. We want to show you what they go through by carrying the water jugs a fraction of the distance they do every day."

His head tilted. I could tell he had never considered these details.

"So, if I walk with the containers, you will donate money?"

"Yes, the Caterpillar Foundation will donate."

We walked over to the jugs, and he bent down and picked up one in each hand. The look on his face said, "Are you kidding me?" A full five-gallon water jug weighs forty pounds. He was suddenly holding eighty pounds. He stood still for a full ten seconds, processing the weight. Then he made his way down the path. I met him at the end. I set down the jugs, and I reached up my hand to shake his. "Thank you so much for giving someone water," I said. "You made a difference in someone's life tonight."

He didn't let go of my hand. Instead, he held it and knelt to my level.

"I have two girls," he explained. "They couldn't carry one can down that path, let alone for hours every single day." He leaned in and gave me a warm hug and said thank you. As I placed a sticker on his shirt, he asked if he could have two more, for his daughters, so he could explain what other girls go through. I gladly handed him two more stickers.

The truth is, it doesn't take much to gain a clearer picture of what life is like for another person and have our perspective changed by it. While you can't walk in someone's shoes, you should always try. Sometimes it takes picking up a forty-pound jug of water and lugging it a few feet. Or, in my case, trying to eat while reclined in a body cast.

After that first dinner at home following my hip surgeries, when I couldn't see the food on my plate, I had one consuming thought: *It must be so hard to eat when you're blind.* Before that day, I had never considered what life was like for a person without sight. Since then, I've never again overlooked a person who is visually impaired.

When I say you can't walk in another person's shoes, I'm not saying that empathy isn't possible. I'm saying that empathy isn't as difficult as it might seem. You don't *have* to walk in another's shoes to see more clearly what life is like for that person. You have to try, have to feel for one moment the weight she carries. Once you've felt it, you have an opportunity to use that feeling to make a greater impact in another's life, as well as an impact on yourself. This is where your leadership can become a profound force for good.

This is where we need to rethink what we mean when we talk about influence. Is the objective of influence to move someone to do something that serves ourselves? If the answer is yes, we can get by on the sort of influence most marketers use. We don't need relationships, because people are merely pawns that can be moved to win the game.

But if the highest objective of influence is more than marketing effectiveness—if we want our influence to achieve something more than simply getting people to comply—then we have to approach relationships differently. We have to view our influence of others as a path for improving their lives.

If we strive to enter into people's lives through greater intimacy—even allowing ourselves to forget the drive to influence—we will often find that influence comes naturally and unequivocally. In the end, the highest form of influence is based on mutual trust and mutual loyalty. When I know you are for me, you will always have my vote. I will listen to what you have to say. I will follow your lead. I will stand for you.

About two weeks after my dad passed, my family received a condolence card from a local woman my family didn't know. On the inside of the card was a brief, thoughtful line that the manufacturer had printed in a golden font. I couldn't tell you what that line said because the woman who'd sent the card had taken up every last millimeter of white space to share a story she thought we'd want to hear.

Her ten-year-old daughter had been saving up her money to attend a local rare coin auction. There was one particular coin she'd heard would be there, and her heart was set on winning it. When it came time to bid, the girl shot up her paddle. Almost immediately, another man in the audience countered with a higher bid. The girl shot her paddle up again. Again, the man outbid her. This back-and-forth continued for two more rounds until the man's bid exceeded the girl's savings. The woman penning the letter explained that she watched her daughter's face fall when she realized she wasn't going to get the coin after all. The young girl sat somberly as the auctioneer looked around the room and asked for any more bidders.

"Going once," he proclaimed.

"Going twice."

Then suddenly, out of nowhere, another man from the very back shot up his paddle and called out a number doubling the previous man's bid. There was no counter bid after that, and the new bidder won the coin. The girl was so distraught, the woman wrote, that she no longer wanted to stay at the auction even though she had money to spend.

The two stood up and headed to the exit at the back of the room. As they approached the door, the bidder from the back walked up to the little girl. With bright eyes, he leaned down and said, "I believe this is yours." He held out the coin and set it in the girl's small hand.

"That man," the woman wrote, "was Don Sullivan."

My dad.

When I read that line, I sobbed and held the letter tight against my chest for what must have been ten minutes. He was the strongest man I knew, strong enough to see through all the crap and enter into the lives of others he'd never met, not for his own sake but for theirs. He understood the best path to influence. And he modeled it for me over and over.

I eventually set the card down on my bed. "No excuses," I whispered to myself with tears still in my eyes. "No more hesitation."

I was going to enter into others' lives as much as possible, despite the risks, and make as big an impact as one little woman could.

I hope you've come to a similar conclusion about your own potential.

CHAPTER 9

A NEW LINE OF SIGHT

I wonder how often we miss solutions to problems and opportunities for progress because we have the wrong perspective to begin with. Our line of sight is often the only factor that determines whether we see a problem or a solution before us. When you look around at the faces in your primary environments, do you see problems or potential for progress?

Most newly minted sixteen-year-olds run to get their driver's licenses on their birthday. I was having surgery at Johns Hopkins on that day. While my license wasn't on anyone else's radar, it was on mine. Over the next three semesters, I talked to my school counselor several times about taking driver's ed, and each time he insisted there was no need. Eventually, I got so frustrated I brought up the issue with my mom. She was my fixer in all things related to education. She marched down to the high school and told the counselor that I needed to keep moving forward toward driving, even if I didn't have my permit yet. They went back and forth, but he could see she wasn't backing down. Finally, he spilled the beans and told her the real reason the school was concerned with me taking the class: they didn't have a car I could practice with.

At the time, buses didn't have lifts for wheelchairs—and I often was in one because of all my surgeries—so my mom was dropping me off at school, and my dad was picking me up. As we headed home one day during my senior year, shortly after my mom's discussion with the counselor, I saw this beautiful, royal blue '74 Mustang in a parking lot with a For Sale sign on it. I was in love.

"Dad, stop!" I ordered. "Pull in!"

He didn't know what I wanted, but he pulled into the lot anyway.

"Look, Dad. Isn't that a beautiful car? That's *my* car! Let's call the number."

My dad knew the time had come to put me in a car, and I'd saved enough to buy one. After a few subsequent phone calls, and a couple of daddy-daughter talks, my dad agreed I could buy the car.

Over the next three weeks, my dad got the Mustang ready for me. He propped up the seat, added extensions to the pedals, and installed a smaller steering wheel. Then came the gearshift. Not only could I not reach it, but my hand wasn't strong enough to push the button that would move it. My dad tried various modifications, and nothing seemed to work.

"I'm not worried, Dad," I told him. "You can fix anything."

At last, the day came. My dad found me in my room on a Saturday and said, "Do you want to sit in your car?"

Oh my gosh!!!

I double-turtled out front and opened the car door. My car was gorgeous. I got in. He jumped in on the other side, a piece of toast in his hand. Then I looked down at the gearshift.

"What is that?"

"A door hinge," he said dryly, as though it was the most obvious modification in the world. He took a bite of toast.

I'd like to tell you I understood how it worked, but I'd be making it up. What I know is that it was a long, black, triangular door hinge, like you might see on an old European door, and when I "opened" the hinge to the right, the other flap of the hinge pushed in the shifter button so I could slide the car into gear. Clearly, there were other spare parts in the assembly, but I have no idea what they were. All I know is that he demonstrated it once, and it worked. Then I did it.

"Leverage," he said, chewing another bite of toast.

"I *love* leverage!" I exclaimed. "Let's go for a spin."

Off we went. I couldn't believe it was happening. My dad told me to pull onto the highway. So, I did. He said to pull onto the next street. I passed the street and kept driving.

"Where are you going?"

"I'm going for a stroll," I said wryly.

I drove around for about twenty minutes. My dad was shocked at how much I knew and how well I did. Over the next few months, my dad helped me hone my skills. It was a rite of passage, even though I was now eighteen. Before long, it was time to get my license.

On a Saturday morning shortly thereafter, my mom and I drove the 'stang to the DMV. I walked in and went to get a number. The dispenser was way over my head. I asked a gentleman nearby to please grab me a number.

"Little girl, where is your parent?" he asked.

"Over there," I said, pointing to my mom. "I'm here to get my license."

He looked me up and down, then hesitantly handed me a number.

As I waited my turn, my leg was bouncing up and down. My number was called and I walked to the counter, also way over my head. I stepped back about five feet, held up my number, and said, "I'm ready!"

I hadn't seen someone so stunned in all my life. Her reaction was much worse than the lady's at the chess tournament. She stood there staring at me. Finally, she said, "What are you here for?"

I told her, and by this point all four people behind the counter were standing next to the woman and staring at me. I was too excited to care.

"What's first?" I asked.

The woman handed me the written test. Aced it. Then the four DMV workers got in an impromptu huddle. I'm not kidding. They were discussing what to do next, because clearly I was not going to take the driving portion of the test.

"We need to do the eye test next," the woman said.

The machine was on top of the counter. No way I was going to reach it. The lady didn't know what to do.

"What if we put it on a chair behind the counter," I suggested, "and then I can reach it?"

She turned around and asked a male employee to move the machine for her. I disappeared behind the counter to take the test. Again, aced it. Time for the driving test!

The woman told me to have a seat and my name would

be called. I was squirming in my chair with excitement. Time went by, and by, and I noticed people were being called up who'd come in after me. I could see the supervisor talking to the people administering the driving tests. He'd say something, and then they would all look at me. I smiled and waved. After thirty minutes, I walked up to the woman and asked if there was a problem.

"No. No, there's no problem."

"Then why are you processing other people ahead of me who had numbers after mine?"

She gave me no answer except that they'd call me soon.

When a man called my name, I flew up to meet him. He asked where my car was, and I walked outside with him to show him the Mustang. He opened the driver door and looked at my dad's modifications. His eyebrows were the only thing that moved.

"Shall we go?" I said.

He nodded and walked around to the passenger seat. I think he might have been saying a final prayer. He probably wondered if he'd make it back.

He said nothing except, "Turn right out of the parking lot."

I started the car, used Dad's "leverage" to put the car in reverse and then drive, and I pulled out of the parking lot. I made three more rights at the man's instruction, and we were back in the parking lot. We drove around the block. No kidding, it took about two minutes. It was so quick that I pulled back into my same parking spot.

"Is that all?" I asked.

"You passed," he said, and then got out of the car and walked straight back into the building without waiting for me.

I didn't care. I ran in to my mom and exclaimed, "I PASSED!"

My mom looked at me with furrowed brows. I nodded. To this day my mom jokes it was the all-time shortest driving test in history.

My final task was posing for my license picture. Another man walked up to me and told me where to sit for the picture. There was a monitor on the back of the camera where you could see how the photo would look. As I sat down, I immediately disappeared from the screen. I started to laugh.

"My, don't I have a blank look," I giggled.

The man's eyes widened to saucer size. He looked horrified.

"How are we going to get a picture?" he blurted out louder than he'd meant to, like you sometimes do with headphones on.

"What if I stand on the chair?"

"That might work," he said, still visibly shaken at his primal outburst.

It did work, and shortly thereafter my license was ready. I must have stared at it for five full minutes before my mom said, "Are you ready to go?"

We jumped back into the car, and this time I was in the driver's seat.

I think back on that story often, and I share it because it's always a reminder of how limited we are when our focus is off-kilter. The DMV employees saw only my differences, and my differences were a problem. They were so focused on them, in fact, that they couldn't even find the resources to solve a simple problem like pulling up a chair or lowering the camera. Perhaps the worst—though I didn't mind the truncated test at all—was the man who'd administered the driver's test. He could not do his job because his perspective on me was so shortsighted.

In 2011, the presidency of Caterpillar's storied foundation became vacant. It wasn't a job with high turnover. The sudden opening became the primary watercooler conversation around the office. It was a position that many wanted. The foundation was investing millions every year to worthy grantees who were helping solve global problems like poverty, hunger, lack of education, and inaccessibility to clean water. It was the president's job to steward those funds compassionately and wisely. It was my dream job.

Having worked in various for-profit roles within the company, I didn't have the expected résumé. And no woman, let alone a disabled one, had ever held the post. I still believed I was more than capable. Most of all, I felt I had the right perspective. I had been looking up at those who had looked down at me all my life. I had learned that while I can't control how people see me, I can always control how I see them. I hoped that, this time, someone was looking up to me.

Unbeknownst to me, Leslie, my boss, wrote to the hiring manager, Jim, requesting that I be considered for the position. When she told me what she'd done, hope swelled up in me. Maybe I had a chance? When Jim read the email, he later confessed he hadn't thought of me at that point, but then a light bulb came on. *Of course!* he thought. *Michele makes perfect sense.*

As the ensuing weeks passed and Jim reviewed hundreds of other applicants—people he called "highly qualified"—he kept circling back to me. When it came time to offer the position, a board meeting was held, where the top recommendations would be discussed. I was still on the list.

The day before the meeting, Doug, Caterpillar's CEO, left Jim a glowing message about me, one that Jim later played for me. "She's the one," Doug insisted on the recording. "To not hire her would be a mistake. She will elevate the foundation to another level."

When Jim called me to share the good news that I had been selected for the position, I tried to hold it together. I'd done a lot in my career, more than anyone ever thought I could, but being trusted with this enormous responsibility was the pinnacle of my career.

I thanked Jim profusely and probably embarrassed myself a bit, but Jim understood. It was an emotional moment for him too. He later told me it was the most important hire he'd made in his career, and that he couldn't wait to break the news to me. Jim asked me to come to his office the next morning, which I did, and there he played for me the whole message he'd received from our CEO. It was like Doug was talking about someone else. Only he wasn't.

It was one of the greatest moments in my life, not just because the position was my dream job but because I realized they saw me worthy of such an impactful role. Leslie, my boss, and these two great men, Jim and Doug, were looking up to me. They saw me. I only wished my dad were there to celebrate with me. When I saw my mom that night, I sobbed.

When I woke up the next morning, I was ready to get to work.

My first overseas trip for the foundation included a visit to a school for disabled children in Tanzania. I met a sixteen-year-old boy named Godlisten, who was born in the village of Oldupai, in the Ngorongoro District of northern Tanzania.

His home is not far from Oldupai Gorge, the famous archaeological site where what are believed to be the oldest human remains were discovered. Godlisten is the oldest of eight children from a traditional Maasai family that is very poor, eking out a small income by raising and selling cows and sheep. Poverty wasn't his biggest challenge. He was born without a left hand and with only one finger on his right hand. The birth defect brought about tragic conflict with his parents. His father believed it was a curse, as is the custom in Tanzania. He blamed and verbally abused both Godlisten and his mother for years.

Eventually, his father could not live under the same roof as his disabled son, for whom he blamed the family's constant economic struggles. Godlisten's father drove him miles from their home and left him at a Roman Catholic rehabilitation center. Godlisten was twelve years old. It would seem the boy had little value and no future. He had no education and as far as anyone knew, no aspirations. The rehabilitation center turned him over to the Faraja Primary School—a facility at the base of Mount Kilimanjaro designed to educate and rehabilitate the spirits of disabled children. When I met Godlisten shortly after he joined the school, he was surrounded by people with a different perspective than his father's, and the resources to change the course of his life.

The school's beginnings can be traced back to an unlikely trip taken by a retired couple from Virginia, Don and Joann Tolmie. Don was an attorney in the railroad industry for four decades. When he retired in his early sixties, he and Joann began to travel the world to experience different cultures. Africa was on their list. In 1999, the Tolmies joined a group of people from a Lutheran church in Virginia to visit Tanzania in cooperation with the Northern Tanzania Diocese of the Lutheran Church, which still had a presence in a small village there. By this time, Don was seventy and Joann was sixty-eight.

The arrangement was that the people of the Tanzanian church would tour them around the country. The rural roads in Tanzania are not very good. Many routes look more like dry riverbeds than dirt lanes. As a result, travel time is often slow. Forty miles can take two to three hours if any portion of the drive is on undeveloped roads. This was the case one day about halfway into the Tolmies' trip.

One morning, they left the southeast corner of Serengeti National Park and headed east toward Arusha on the A23, arriving at a small town on the southwestern border of Mount Kilimanjaro National Park, called Sanya Juu. From there they turned onto a three-mile dry-riverbed of a road that was so rocky and kicked up so much dust they had to drive ten miles per hour and keep a quarter-mile separation between their van and the next vehicle. The road rose on a slow incline, and dotting either side every half mile or so were small houses made of mud and sticks, with thatched or corrugated roofs. Surrounding the homes was farmland occupied by crops, and large swaths of hilly, yellow-green fields where the Maasai take their cows and goats to graze.

Toward the end of the three-mile ride, the Tolmies' van crested a small hill and the landscape opened up. In the distance just beyond a grouping of trees was a small building of basic cinder-block construction. The Tolmies were told it was a vocational training center where disabled young adults were learning trades, from tailoring and carpentry to welding and jewelry making. Don and Joann stepped from the van with their hosts and walked inside. There weren't more than a dozen students.

Joann was instantly drawn to the place. Her mother, a woman named Mabel Swanson, was a teacher in Rock Island, Illinois. When she was widowed at thirty-four, she doubled down on her work as an instructor of what back then they called the "crippled children's class." Every child with a physical disability in Rock Island's entire district was in the same classroom. For the remainder of her career, Mabel taught twenty to twenty-five students every weekday, some with severe disabilities. It became her life's passion.

After the loss of their father, Joann and her brother spent much of their time with their mother in that classroom. In time, they came to see that, despite the physical challenges of their mother's students and the pervasive belief that disabled children had no future, these students were no different from able-bodied students. They felt the same emotions, wondered the same things about the world, and dreamed the same life dreams. Many were brilliant. All had great value.

When looking at the disabled Tanzanians, Joann saw the faces of her mother's students, whom she'd gotten to know when she was a girl. She began to ask questions.

A Tanzanian deacon spoke up. "It's very difficult for us to get them here," he admitted. "They must have primary school education first." He then explained that in the rural areas there wasn't a single primary school in Tanzania for the physically disabled.

"We do have a farm that was donated to us," he continued,

"and on that farm we have built a training center for deacons. We have a set of plans for a primary school for the disabled, but we have not been able to build it. We've been waiting for someone to come and help make this a reality."

"How long have you been waiting?" asked Don.

"For five years," the deacon replied.

It was a stirring moment for the Tolmies. Their travel plans during retirement entailed seeing the world, interacting with new cultures, and appreciating people in new ways. They weren't looking for a specific opportunity. But now one was before them. The deacon hadn't directly asked them or even insinuated that the Tolmies were the people they'd been waiting for. In her spirit, however, Joann felt a tug. She'd seen the hopeful eyes of the beautiful young adults there. She'd watched them learning. She knew.

Don and Joann returned home the following week and began considering whether they could help make the primary school a reality. They weighed everything from the financial aspect of it to the logistics of doing work in Tanzania and their ages. They also brought their three boys into the discussion. They asked, "Is this possible? Are we too old to take on a project so far away?" They didn't want to offer a hope they couldn't fulfill. Ultimately, their sons encouraged them to proceed. They, their wives, and their children would all join in. They agreed they could not ignore what they'd seen.

For the next several months, the Tolmies, three generations of them ranging from middle schoolers to the early seventies, raised money to build the school. In rural Tanzania, the labor and unadorned raw materials like cinder block are a fraction of what they would cost in the States, but it was real money and it was also just the beginning. There would be the costs for room and board for every student, along with the expense of books, teachers, supplies, and ongoing maintenance. That is, if the school worked out. The Tolmies were all in regardless.

In July 2001, the school broke ground with sixteen students. They named it Faraja, which means "comfort" in Swahili. In 2008, Faraja celebrated its first graduating class of fifteen students. The joy and pride in the students' families is moving to witness. But not as moving as the joy and pride in the students themselves.

At Faraja, students are taught to look for opportunities to serve one another. All hands are always available to help. They cook; they clean; they lift each other into wheelchairs and onto beds. I once watched a ten-year-old girl with a deformed foot set down her food at lunchtime to push her friend who was in a wheelchair and unable to move quickly on his own. She dragged her foot along in the dirt as she pushed. Both wore huge grins. Time spent at the school opens your eyes, if they weren't already open when you arrived there.

When the Tolmies first raised the funds to build the school, their agreement with the school and the local Lutheran church was that they would fund a majority percentage of the operating costs for the first two years. The hope was that with a combination of the Tanzanian government's assistance that they had arranged and the support of local families, the local community would eventually take over completely. Neither Don and Joann nor their sons' families envisioned the growth that would occur.

The more time the Tolmies spent with the students each

year, the more they realized there were other ways they could enter in. Since its inception, the Faraja School has added medical care, social and recreational activities, physical therapy, and occupational and extracurricular skills, like computer and agricultural training. Let's just say that the initial commitment is not the same as the current commitment. The budget is ten times what the Tolmies thought it was going to be. They are fine with this because the outcomes in the students' lives are ten times ten. The same return is evident in the Tolmies' lives.

Don is adamant that he and Joann don't run the school; the Tanzanians run the school. He recently told the headmaster that if he ever shows up and finds the Tolmie name painted on a building, he will do two things. First, he will find a can of white spray paint and cover their names. Second, he will never come back. The headmaster laughed, but Don's point was made.

There's a small renovation currently happening at the school. Portions of the buildings are being repainted and repaired for structural wear and tear. I recently received some pictures of the progress. A description has been painted in black on the outside of the main white cinder-block school building. It reads "The Faraja Primary School for the Physically Disabled. Built in honor of Mabel Swanson." I laughed when I saw it; the clever Tanzanians still figured out a way to honor Don and Joann without using the Tolmie name.

Three generations of Tolmies now serve with the leaders at Faraja, helping in areas such as national controls, fiscal discipline, and thoughtful planning. Each of the eight grandchildren has paid the school multiple visits and remains actively involved despite living in the States. Maddie, a

twenty-eight-year-old MBA student at the University of
Michigan, is a great example. She chairs the Faraja Youth
Board, which recently raised enough money to provide Faraja
with a new computer lab, complete with twenty-one new computers. The effects of good vision are deep and wide.

Don and Joann made thirty-six total trips together over
the years. When they made their final trip to Faraja, approximately two years ago, at eighty-eight and eighty-six years
old, dozens rushed to the arriving van, calling out "Bibi!" and
"Babu!"—Swahili for grandmother and grandfather. It was
not just the students who used those names; it was the deacons
and elders of the church; it was the teachers, the headmaster,
and the bishop. Don and Joann are revered, and the reverence
goes both ways. The Tolmies have always looked up to the
beautiful people at Faraja, as Faraja now looks up to them.

For Don's ninetieth birthday, the Tolmies had eighteen
fruit trees planted along each side of a path that connects
the school buildings to the chapel, one tree for every Tolmie
child, grandchild, and great-grandchild. The Tanzanians
named the path Bibi and Babu Way. In due time, the elder
Tolmies' bodies will fail them, but the trees will bear fruit
that will continue to nourish the students, as the students'
lives will bear fruit that will nourish their families, their communities, and even the world.

There's an expression in the Tolmie family that has been
passed down from generation to generation: "Live beyond
yourself." A small round stone inscribed with this phrase sits
at the home of Dave Tolmie, the oldest of Don and Joann's
three sons. The stone is a reminder of the ripple effect of
true, clear vision. Like a body of water when a pebble is

dropped in, small waves of impact roll outward. More eyes are opened. More leaders are made. More people are seen. Lives are elevated—at home and abroad. Sometimes these are lives that were in greater danger than anyone realized.

The disenfranchised in Tanzania face a bleak future. Tanzanian students who were born albino—"albeeno," as the locals say—attend schools with huge walls skirting the land on which they sit, like a medieval fortress. Outside those walls, albino students would be hunted down and chopped up for body parts to sell as talismans or good-luck charms. While disabled students aren't hunted, many are treated like the lepers of biblical times. They are outcasts, often required to live outside communities, if not physically so, emotionally so. They are not seen as equals or as whole people but as broken people unworthy of love and attention.

When Faraja's national test scores began to come in, these conclusions were challenged. Standardized tests are given to seventh-grade students in all schools throughout the country to determine whether they are fit to move on to what Africans call "secondary school" (what Americans call middle school). The first class who graduated from Faraja in 2008 scored in the top 5 percent of the entire country. It raised some eyebrows, to say the least. Every year since then, the seventh-grade students at Faraja have continued to score in the top 5 percent. In the past four years, they were in the top 3 percent nationally.

Awareness of the Faraja students' scores has created waves over the last decade. Not only have the communities in Tanzania begun to see disabled people differently, but the Tanzanian government has begun to support the disabled with legislation, such as the requirement that 10 percent of every company's workforce be disabled people. While this doesn't always occur in practice, the fact that it's legislated is an enormous, historical leap that points to a changing national perception, so much so that the Tanzanian prime minister recently visited the school. Shortly thereafter, Don and Joann received a letter from parliament in appreciation for all their work on behalf of disabled students in Tanzania.

You might ask how the improving line of sight plays out in the students' lives. I certainly was asking this as part of the Caterpillar Foundation's grantee criteria. When I visited for the first time, it was an unlikely homecoming. When I rolled out of the van, the students were drawn to me. I wasn't used to that response in Africa. I think in their minds they were thinking, *Wow. How did she get here? She can do the kinds of things that we didn't know somebody who had our kinds of physical challenges could do.* They looked at me as though I were some kind of miracle or superhero. Seeing me changed how they saw themselves. If I could get myself there—dwarfism, scooter, age, and all—certainly there was much more they could do than they even thought possible. I could see the sparkle in their eyes, and it put a sparkle in mine.

I'd brought T-shirts from Bradley University and CAT for some of them—ninety-two students, and six of them born with dwarfism. They put the shirts on and started to dance. I stood from my chair and danced with them.

Normally, when I travel to a country where the foundation has several grantees, I only have time to spend a couple of hours at most, because we have quite a few people to see. I spent the entire day at Faraja. A government official from the region was there to meet me too. The kids showed me the school buildings (now three of them), their rooms where they slept, the kitchen where they prepared the food as a team, and their animals and lush crops in the surrounding fields. Their gardens were composed of raised beds, because many of them cannot bend to the ground. I stepped in poop on the way from the fields to lunch, and we all had a good laugh. An eternal laugh that I believe God and the angels shared with us. I remember thinking right then that the school is an oasis in more ways than one. And I was getting to drink from its spring.

When I left that evening, I told the children I would return. They probably didn't fully comprehend it at their age, but they are more of an inspiration to me than I am to them. In me, they saw possibility. In them, I see life.

Godlisten graduated two years ago. He's now finishing business school, with plans to start a small business grinding maize into cornmeal and selling it to the Ngorongoro Region, where the meal is scarce but needed. The Faraja Fund Foundation has already provided Godlisten a small business loan to get him started. The proceeds from the business will allow his seven siblings to go to school, something his parents aren't able to afford. None of his siblings have a physical disability like he does. In Godlisten, we can see a miraculous paradox: a brother born without hands offering to his siblings a helping hand that no one else in the family can. But is this turn of events such a reach? It's not when *how* a person sees is highly valued. The right line of sight toward others is a potent force.

When we judge people or see them as unworthy or incapable, we deny that we are all equal in the eyes of God. Do you believe this? It takes an otherworldly grace to see others in this way, but we have access to it. I love when a poor line of sight is proven faulty, as it was that day in the DMV. I bet you like it too—even when it's our own vision that needs an adjustment. To have our eyes opened to the beauty and potential in another person is one of the greatest experiences in life. Think of your favorite movies, books, and TV shows. Aren't the most moving, memorable scenes the ones where the underdog overcame, where the weak became strong, where the least became the first? Do you know why that is? Redemption is built into our beings. It is the gravity of our souls. We feel it when we see it. We experience it more often when we see it outside our own experiences.

Recently the Tolmies brought a visitor to Faraja, a man who holds one of the fastest ascents and descents of Mount Kilimanjaro in history. Godlisten took to the man instantly. Ever since he came to Faraja as an underestimated teenage boy, he'd been storing up in his heart a dream to climb the beautiful snowcapped mountain he could see every day in the distance. He shared his dream with the man that day. Not long after that, the man returned and the two fulfilled Godlisten's dream. When I heard the news, I was ecstatic. I also thought, *It's not the first mountain he's climbed. And it won't be the tallest. He will climb so much higher.*

Today, Godlisten is a tall, handsome young man on his way to owning his own business. He's also a brilliant artist. These two accomplishments alone are more than anyone ever thought possible. But his greatest accomplishment to date is his vision. All along, his greatest dream has been to pay for his siblings' education. Despite all the hell he's been through, he still sees them. I recently heard that his father has begun to come around. Perhaps one day he, too, will see as his son sees.

I've been around the world now, visiting nearly every continent on behalf of the Caterpillar Foundation. It is clear there are opportunities both abroad and at home to take initiative and enter into the lives of others, to see past their limitations, learn their perspectives, and use leadership for lasting impact. The question isn't so much, Where are the opportunities? as it is, Which side of those opportunities are you on?

But the truth is, your answer to both questions comes down to your line of sight. If you're looking up to others, you'll not only see more opportunities—you'll also be in prime position to seize them.

We all have reasons for people to underestimate, overlook, and misunderstand us. For most people, these reasons can be hidden or removed. For others, including me, some differences are impossible to hide. I can honestly say I'm grateful for this. Like my favorite nurse, Kathy, taught me, I've learned to accept my limitations and get on with life. My limitations have also taught me the link between perspective and impact. How you see is a direct measure of the impact you can achieve in the lives of others. The more you see, the more you can achieve. The more people who see, the more *we* can achieve.

Earlier, I didn't tell you that my little airplane bathroom incident with my fellow passenger was on my way to the 2015 World Economic Forum. While it was an honor to be invited and join some three thousand of the world's most prominent economists, businesspeople, celebrities, and heads of state, that little incident was a foreshadowing of the dichotomy of the next four days. On one hand, the landscape of the Swiss

Alps isn't exactly suited for a four-foot-tall woman rocking a scooter. On the other hand, since Davos is where many of the world's elite congregate, I had an ideal place to learn how the people in positions of influence are seeing.

One afternoon, on our way to a meeting of major business leaders, my friend J. R. and I made our way through the ice and snow to the hotel where the forum was being held. I needed to use the ladies' room, and by now you might assume I had learned my lesson. But you'd be wrong.

I walked into the big, clean, empty bathroom I wished I'd had on the plane ride over. I admired the space a moment and then entered a stall that featured a self-locking latch. It's a fantastic feature for anyone but me. I couldn't reach the latch or squeeze under the stall walls. A half hour later, J. R.'s phone finally had reception, and my call from the stall came through. I'll just say that it wasn't my first call. J. R., if you haven't already it figured out, is a man, so he found a woman nearby and asked her to save me. (I would've loved to hear that conversation.) The woman was very gracious, and I was freed in under a minute.

I offered a thumbs-up and a Cheshire cat grin to J. R. once I reappeared. He shook his head. He then navigated us aboard a nearby elevator, where we promptly got stuck—for another thirty minutes. Incidentally, Swiss hotel elevators are smaller than airplane bathrooms. Thank God I'm not claustrophobic.

All told, it took us an hour and a half to get to that important meeting. I felt like we'd climbed the Matterhorn by the time we arrived. The discussion was already underway as we slid into the room. The meeting featured the great work several organizations were doing to make education available to people living in poverty. Our tardiness landed us a spot next to Bill Gates, who leaned over to me a few minutes later and said, "Michele, you're ahead of us in this." He was referring to our partnership with Global Poverty Project, which advocates for those living in extreme poverty. It was one of my prouder moments. Bill and his wife, Melinda, are changing lives around the world, particularly in impoverished communities. To receive such a compliment from him was high praise. Suddenly, the challenges to getting there didn't matter—not just there in that Davos hotel but there at that point in my life.

I could honestly say then, and still can say today, that a lifetime of disability is worth the potent perspective it has given me. But you don't have to be in my shoes to look up to others everywhere you go and in everything you do. You have to grasp that *how* you see always frames *who* you see.

And you have to ask yourself: Does my line of sight equip me to make an immediate impact on others?

Differences and difficulties shrink when your sightline is pointed at making an impact. Especially because there is always another person to see, and more work to do.

You have to grasp that how *you see always frames* who *you see.*

Dave Tolmie, Don and Joann's oldest son, was in Tanzania with his parents, wife, and three kids in 2003, not long after the school had broken ground and before the standardized testing had begun to prove the vision worthy. Dave's family was staying at a hotel owned by the Lutheran church, down the hill from Faraja. The breakfasts are picnic-style seating, and Dave and his ten-year-old son were eating early, before many others had arrived, when an African pastor wearing a clerical collar walked up.

"Is there anybody sitting here?" he asked kindly.

Dave told him no and welcomed him to join them.

As the man sat down, he asked, "Are you with that group from Virginia?"

"We are," Dave replied.

"I have to tell you a story," the man said. "I'm a pastor, and my faith has been shaky. I was losing my way, and I'd heard about this school where the Americans came and they said, 'We will build a school for the disabled.'"

He paused and glanced down at his food before continuing.

"I couldn't understand why they would do that. I wondered, *What do they want from us?* So, I went to this school, and I saw this incredible place, and these students who were being educated and helping each other and filled with love and hope for the future. And I saw that, and I said to the older American couple who was there, 'What do you want from us? Why are you doing this?' A student in a wheelchair with twisted legs and arms was sitting by and listening, and before the couple answered, the young boy said proudly, 'Because they love us.'

"I was so inspired by this experience," the pastor said, his tone more excited now, "that I went back to my church and I gave a sermon about it. And I told the church about this school and this couple and this boy in the wheelchair, and afterward people came up to me and said, 'Who are these people? What do they want from us?' I told them that they don't want anything. They're here because we're all children of God, equal in his sight. It has brought such great renewal of our faith to be reminded of this."

As Dave and his son listened to the pastor, they could only smile. They said nothing about their relationship to the "older couple." Inside they were swelling with pride and gratitude for the ripple that had been created. In the years following that encounter, Dave watched the ripple cross oceans and reach friends and other family members in the States. Business friends would hear the story and be changed. Some who are retired would say, "The first time your parents went they were sixty-eight and seventy? Are you kidding?" And suddenly they'd see there is always time to enter into the lives of others. We are never retired from that work, are we?

When this is your paradigm, you possess an elevated point of view that will send ripples of impact for a lifetime. You won't see all of them. But they are still there, and they will continue rolling.

CHAPTER 10

THE REAL MEASURE OF IMPACT

A friend once reminded me that no matter where you go, whenever you come into contact with another person, you either leave that person a little better or a little worse. We always have an effect on others no matter what the circumstances are. When we see that all other people are valuable, showing them should be the very next step. Doing nothing should never be an option.

The evening of the day I was deliberately shoved to the parking lot pavement outside the ice cream parlor, my mom had explained to me the reality that people often mock or fear what they don't know. After that talk, I had two prominent feelings. The first was, *Holy crap! I have to watch out for people doing this all my life?* I couldn't believe that people sought to harm others simply because they were different. I've accepted it as a harsh reality of life, but I'll never get over my initial shock.

My second thought was, *I can't worry about that.* Even as a little girl, I sensed that a life lived in fear was not really life. It was an edited life, a limited life, a life that couldn't possibly reach its potential because it was and would always be focused on self-preservation. I'm grateful my second thought won out that day and continues to win out into my fifties. I knew and still know that you can't make an impact in your own life or the lives of others without releasing others to the freedom of their own perceptions. In other words, I can only control how I see. You can only control how you see.

But how *you* see can change how *others* see, if your line of sight leads to action.

After that parking-lot incident I became focused on being the kind of person others could respect, if they took the time to see the reasons I was worthy of it. This wasn't limited to my behavior. It included seeing others as I hoped they would see me, no matter who they were and what scenario had put us in one another's presence.

What began as a one-day-at-a-time commitment grew into a proven life philosophy. I came to accept that there will always be people who underestimate me in various ways, some that I can understand and others that I cannot. I've committed to not make the same mistake with them. I've vowed to see with soft, expectant eyes, even with those whose ways are harsh and hard to watch. I hope you will own this commitment with me.

We can't let the misperceptions around us cloud our view. As I grew from a middle school girl into a young adult, I grew

THE REAL MEASURE OF IMPACT

stronger in my ability to see beauty in others, and when I initially couldn't, I sought to bring it out in how I treated them. By the time I headed off to college, I had experienced more than my fair share of the challenges this posed. I still expected life to be easier as a young adult among other young adults.

I was right and I was wrong. My college classmates at Bradley University quickly got to know the real me and made my college and postcollege experience very rewarding. But there was a professor who refused to acknowledge my presence for an entire semester. Every class, I'd pause and say hello to him as I walked past his desk. Every class, he looked away and said nothing in response. I'd met people like him before, but I was still shocked that a man who was paid to lead for a living, a man who held a PhD, could be so blind. Fortunately, he was the lone exception among dozens of phenomenal professors at Bradley.

A few weeks into the semester, I learned that he was trying to have me removed from his class. The head of the department contacted me by phone and asked if I wanted to change classes. I said no thanks and vowed to myself right then that I'd get no less than an A in the class. When I turned in my final assignment and secured that grade, I knew I'd done all I could. I hadn't bowed my vision to his. If a person refuses to see me, that's his problem, not mine. I've decided I will offer grace, not judgment—I'd be a hypocrite to do otherwise. And I'd be turning my back on the legacy that was handed down to me from so many who came before me.

An interesting detail about that experience with the professor is that while he refused to see me, there was, unbeknownst to me, someone in that class who did the precise opposite. His name was John, and he turned out to be the husband of a woman named Lisa, who would find herself interviewing me for a promotion at CAT four years later.

The interview went as many job interviews go with me: encouragingly but with some uncertainty about how I came across. Did I come on too strong or not speak up enough? This time I was worried I hadn't spoken up enough. I worried Lisa would see me as someone who still needed to learn to take more initiative or be a better leader. I didn't know this was the case, but it was how I felt.

Lisa went home the evening after the interview and told her husband about me. She never gave me the details of what she said to him, but she did tell me that when John heard "little person" and my name, he knew who his wife was talking about. He then recounted to her what he'd witnessed in that classroom at Bradley University years before. He saw that the professor was stubborn, biased, and even cruel. He explained that the professor had never once made eye contact with me that he knew of. I thought I was the only one who noticed. But someone else was watching. I was as grateful to hear that story as I was to receive the promotion the following week. There is tremendous delight in being seen.

A few years ago, I visited a school in a region of Rwanda that had received funds from the Global Partnership for Education (GPE). The GPE supports developing countries to ensure that every child receives a quality basic education. They prioritize those living in the poorest, most vulnerable, and fragile countries.

When our van pulled up to a school, the regional education minister greeted us. The school had five one-story buildings and a playground with a basketball court. Many students were playing basketball. As I rolled up to the court, the playing came to a standstill. I said hello and introduced myself. An older boy walked over and shook my hand with one hand while holding the basketball in the other.

"You really have a nice school here," I told him.

"Yes, we do now," he replied.

"What do you mean?"

"They have expanded the buildings," he explained, "and we even have computers now. Do you have a computer?"

I told him I did.

The young man behind him piped up. "Aren't they fun? They can do so much!"

"They sure are!" I agreed. "What else has changed?"

"We have toilets!" the first boy exclaimed as he pointed to a building we'd passed on the way in. He then asked if I could stay and watch them play basketball for a few minutes. Of course I could.

Afterward I joined the minister of education on a tour. At the conclusion of the tour, a half dozen of us sat in a classroom while the minister told us the school's story. (I loved the smaller desks!)

The students hadn't been attending school, and those who did weren't doing well. It wasn't their fault. They didn't have textbooks. They didn't have qualified teachers. There was no outreach to get students to the schools in the first place. I could see the pain in the minister's eyes as he confessed that the region's leaders had failed the young people.

He stared at the floor. "It was my job to find resources to help them."

He explained that he'd reached out to the government and discovered GPE. It took a couple of years to see progress in their outreach to families whose support they needed to get the kids to school. Parents began to see the notable progress in the local children. The vision spread. Attendance grew, the number of classrooms grew, and so did the support of GPE. You could see the education minister's pride swelling when he revealed that 98 percent of the children in their region were now in school, and the majority of secondary students were going on to an advanced education.

As I listened to his story, I couldn't help but think of how all progress starts with one person looking up, but it's often slow, unrecognized progress until multiple parties look up together. There was no question that he cared about the children in his region. In fact, he felt responsible for the situation getting as bad as it had. At some point, his vision became clear. He saw the children. He saw their potential, and he saw his integral role in the matter. But he still needed someone to see *him* in order for his vision to become a reality. He also needed others to share in his vision. I asked myself: *How do we know when multiple parties are invested? How do we know if enough people are seeing what needs to be seen?* After all, we can't see how others are seeing. As I can't walk in your shoes, I can't see through your eyes.

This was something I spent months thinking through after I took over the Caterpillar Foundation. In the end, I determined four things: (1) collaboration is key; (2) we have to measure impact, not output; (3) we need to determine root causes and address them; and (4) we have to work from grass-tops to grassroots.

People say that seeing is believing. I say that when it comes to believing in others, seeing is doing. Anyone can be moved by a film, website, or flyer and say a prayer. Anyone can write a check. Anyone can take a trip. What the world needs now is people who keep their eyes on the end goal until it's reached.

One of my first orders of business at the foundation was reframing the way we operated. I knew it would cause quite a stir, but now that the role was mine, I was going to make some changes. The foundation board, my team, and I set an aspirational eight-year goal: to impact the lives of fifty million people living in poverty. That meant different things to different people. To me, it meant life change, seeing families no longer living in the poverty that had plagued them for generations. It meant seeing children not only going to school but also graduating into a job that allowed them to provide for their families. It meant not only building wells in desperate areas but also ensuring that the girls who'd been spending every day gathering water were now being educated, and that the communities who used the wells were getting healthier and children were no longer dying from waterborne disease.

I needed a way to track this sort of impact. My math brain came full scale. I spent the first few months observing how things operated. I wanted to understand the elements that worked and uncover areas where we could improve. More than anything, I wanted to know where I could best serve the foundation's mission to impact the lives of those in poverty. It's easy to assume a company like Caterpillar has unlimited resources. While the company has a lot to give from a financial standpoint, the two critical resources money can't provide are the right vision and the right partnerships. I needed individuals with perspectives that compelled them to collaborate with us to carry out the work that needed to be done.

My primary role as president was determining the strategy for investing millions in grant money every year to create sustainable change in individual lives. I took maximizing every single dollar very seriously. In 2012, I rolled out a new operational strategy for the foundation that fundamentally changed how we measured ROI (return on investment). Typically, foundations and their grantees measure returns by output—for example, how many schools were built or how many microloans were issued. While this certainly measures the productivity of a foundation and isn't irrelevant, I don't believe it measures actual, long-term impact. I wanted our foundation to always have a sense for what grants had the greatest impact and how many lives were truly elevated by our investments. This meant creating a metric to track details such as how many recipients of microloans broke their family's cycle of poverty. Knowing that sort of data would tell us how much impact we were having. This new strategy meant new grantee reporting rules around the measurement of outcome instead of output.

It was a stark change for many of our grantees. Dozens of calls, letters, and emails came in from nonprofits who were not accustomed to the changes. Our team worked with these organizations to help them create the right metrics. Eventually, their perspectives changed when their ability to prove that impact was occurring opened up additional funding from sources who required this data.

Another operational detail that became apparent to me was that certain grants were repeated year after year, without confirming the ongoing effectiveness of our investments. This seemed to me a nearsighted approach. While it would have been much easier to keep writing the checks, I wanted to honor our commitment to fostering long-term relationships and felt this required verifying that we were investing in these relationships the right way, especially when fighting a tough battle like poverty. Essentially, I wanted to know if we were defeating it and, if not, what needed to change? What more did we need to see or understand?

Through hands-on research, asking lots of questions, and spending time with both our grantees and the individuals they were helping, it became clear that as the woman goes, so goes the family. If women are documented from birth, educated, given support for their businesses, and married after becoming an adult, their chances of success are exponentially greater, and their family follows suit. With this knowledge, we created a proprietary collaborative platform known as Together.Stronger. Its name reveals the core initiative: ToGetHer Stronger. The objective became a pillar of our investments and emphasizes monetary accountability—dollar-to-impact behavior—and strategic alliances across public, private, and nonprofit sectors. I knew we couldn't singlehandedly see and help 50 million people. Our partners make the impact.

One year after I took over, we contributed a grant to Water.org to expand its microfinance program, WaterCredit, which allows families in poverty to borrow money to purchase toilets or get clean water piped into their homes. The initial effect was that the number of people who gained access to clean water jumped to 3.2 million. We didn't stop there, however. We connected Water.org with Opportunity International, one of our other partners, to increase capital to provide more WaterCredit loans. The vision to bring water to all the beautiful people who desperately needed it wasn't mine. It was the vision of Matt Damon and Gary White. It wasn't my vision to provide microloans to help people start farms and businesses and meet basic needs. It was the vision of Al Whittaker, former president of Bristol Myers International Corporation, and Australian entrepreneur David Bussau. It wasn't even my vision to build the world's largest construction equipment manufacturer. I just worked there. But I knew how to look up to people. Together with a few others who also knew how, we were able to bring about exponential change well beyond the number of people our personal vision could reach. Today, Water.org has helped 22 million people access clean water. Opportunity International has provided financial products to over 10 million people in more than twenty countries.

For our vision to have its biggest impact, we have to trade credit and recognition for collaboration. After all, looking up to others is about them, not us.

The change in approach was never about bureaucracy or introducing more red tape into the process. It certainly wasn't about control. It was about the need to stop generalizing our approach to how we help people. It was also about introducing accountability into our efforts so we know that seeing people and their circumstances doesn't end with merely feeling empathy. It was ultimately about stewardship of vision—making the best use of the insight we'd been given into every single life: male or female; a retired, white

American attorney or a single African American mother. Over the years, many modeled for me this conviction about stewardship, but my mom is at the top of the list. She continues to see me and step in to see with me whenever necessary. I don't know that she's ever considered how much her insight into my life was one of the initial dominoes of all the progress that's occurred since I was just a little girl born with dwarfism and big dreams.

As I was finishing up this book, my mom and I stayed together in a house on the beach in Florida. We had a lot of time to reminisce. We laughed a lot and shed some tears too. One evening we were trying to recall the few times she'd ever lost her cool (a necessity sometimes). She's never great about remembering these moments—on purpose, I think— but there's one I'll never forget. It was the day I nearly lost my life and dignity in one fell swoop.

I'd like to tell you it occurred while I was shoving an elderly woman from the path of an oncoming bus, but unfortunately, what happened is slightly less heroic. Okay, it's not heroic at all. Two months after my forty-fourth birthday, I lost my balance in my bathroom. I fell backward onto the wood floor and heard a crack in my neck. I immediately knew what had happened. My body went numb. I was able to move, but barely. I managed to get ahold of my cell phone and call my mom, who called 911. Before I knew it, I was being strapped to a gurney and lifted into an ambulance. I closed my eyes on the way to the hospital and slipped into a sort of dreamful state. I thought of what would become of my life. Was this how I was going to die? I saw flashbacks of my childhood. As I felt I was spiraling into my final moment, I felt God's assurance that I'd be okay and that my purpose in life had not yet been fulfilled. I immediately woke up.

I looked at the EMTs and said, "My neck is broken—the C6 vertebra."

At that point I'd spent more time in the hospital than most medical students. I knew my body well.

The EMTs laughed.

"Your neck's fine," one of them said wryly. "It's clearly not broken."

"I know it's broken," I insisted. "And I need to be seen by a spine specialist as soon as we get to the ER."

"Just relax," one of them said through a grin. I could tell they thought it was hilarious I was self-diagnosing. How dare I know my own body?

Two hours later, I was in a halo with a resident physician in charge of my care. I have no problem with medical professionals who are finishing up their school—remember that Kathy was a nursing student when I met her—but this particular resident was rather fond of his newly acquired title. He was the exact opposite of Kathy.

I don't know if you've ever had one of those metal halos installed on your head, but I need to tell you it's your worst nightmare. We're talking four sharp screws tightened into your skull—drilled through your skin and into bone. As though I hadn't already suffered enough, I had trouble with my first halo. Despite the doctor twisting those screws into my head like he was popping a zit, the halo kept coming loose. The first time it happened, the resident didn't assume it was me who had done it. He screwed it back in. Oh, the joy of a second time around. I was hollering the entire time. He was sweating but doggone it, he was going to get those screws in there permanently this time. The scene was so traumatic my mom had to step out of the room.

When it was done, it was done. There's nothing more to say. I survived. Then the halo came loose again. This time the resident took it personally. His posture said I was to blame, and how dare I ruin his bloody masterpiece a second time. He made his displeasure known. I gave it right back to him.

"This isn't working," I said.

"You can't move around so much," he shot back. "I don't know how you're doing this."

"I'm not doing anything!" I yelled.

Eventually he stopped talking to me and began trying to screw the thing back in a third time. The pain was excruciating. Same wounds, new screws, take three.

"I'm not doing this again!" I yelled. "STOP! You're killing me!"

I couldn't take it anymore. I told him not to touch my head. He stepped back, highly offended, like I'd smacked him.

"You have to have your neck stabilized," he demanded.

"I agree. But it's not happening with a halo. You go and figure out another option. This obviously isn't working."

He stormed out and blew past my mom, who was listening from the hallway.

The following morning, two gentlemen from the prosthetics department arrived with a different type of brace. No screws! While it was more confining than the halo, it did the job, and there wasn't anything that could come loose. I also had four fewer holes in my head.

That resident doctor was never going to see me. And we

can't force people to see us or others. But we shouldn't let this dissuade us from collaborating openly. I firmly believe this planet is made up of a lot of good people who, when given the opportunity to look up, can correct their line of sight and join with a collective vision.

It is a huge mistake to take a defensive approach to making an impact, choosing to help only this person or that person, declaring you'll only work with this type of individual but not that one, casting your glance only at those who look like you. If I've learned anything about impactful collaboration at the highest levels, I've learned it requires stakeholders from both the grasstops and the grassroots.

The first question I had to ask myself when I accepted the leadership of the Caterpillar Foundation was not, as some might have assumed, Where should we invest the money? It was, How should we invest the money? My answer was that we should combine the financial advantages of the grasstops with the activist advantages of the grassroots. The combination can be catalytic if the people involved continue to look up to others, including those with whom they're collaborating.

In 2017, I was at a ONE Foundation board meeting with Bono and other board members. As you might imagine, these meetings are very involved and often stretch from early morning until late at night, two days in a row. The work ONE is doing is significant and very important to all of us involved, so there's always much to discuss and decide.

During the latest meeting, we'd taken a ten-minute bathroom break after five straight hours of conversation. Bono was particularly dragging that day, as he'd come off a tour the day before. Not wanting his energy to be a liability,

THE REAL MEASURE OF IMPACT

he looked over at me—the lone board member who hadn't headed to the bathroom—and said, "Michele, I need you to chase me."

My eyebrows lifted.

"What do you mean, 'chase you'?"

"I need to get my energy up," he said. "I need you to chase me around the room."

I looked at him to verify that he was serious. He was already stretching. Laughing, I said okay and navigated my scooter away from the table and toward him. As I approached, he stood, stretched his arms to the sky, and then started jogging. I accelerated to top speed, which isn't cheetah-like, but it's faster than a stroll, and he picked up his pace accordingly. Round and round we went, me spinning at Bono's heels, and together carving an oval-shaped trail around the edges of the large conference room. We must have been on lap six or seven when the door opened and the others began to file back into the room. Imagine their surprise when instead of seeing two colleagues saddled up to the table, hashing out a serious plan, bladders be damned, they found a motorized little person chasing one of the world's biggest rock stars around the room. I was glad they had some context.

I tell you this story because it's critical we remember that while our efforts to look up to others are very significant, they can and should still remain fun and life-giving. We're just people, after all, siblings in God's family, trying to lift one another up instead of tear one another down. The vital nature of this endeavor should draw out its profound beauty and sense of vitality rather than remove it. Let's take that to heart.

Bono could easily do nothing other than lounge by the

Mediterranean and count the hues of blue and green. However, the one constant in his life, regardless of his demanding schedule, is trying to look up to as many people as his line of sight can possibly reach—to inspire people and policymakers to embrace and support ONE's vision. And not just those far and wide. He's always had a profound knack for seeing the opportunities within arm's length as well.

After our jog around the conference room, the board members took their seats and we jumped back into conversation about ONE's work stateside. About twenty minutes in, Bono was addressing a board member's question about a particular marketing campaign when he stopped midsentence.

"Michele," he said in his strong Irish brogue, "how's your mother?"

She'd recently come out of surgery to install a stent in her coronary artery. I told him that she was slowed up some but on the mend.

"Could I write her a note?" he asked.

"Of course," I replied.

He promptly announced, "Let's pause the meeting," and reached into his satchel and produced a piece of stationery and an envelope. Then he wrote the note, right there, while we waited. It didn't take him more than a couple of minutes, and then he placed the note in the envelope and handed it to me. "Please give this to Bonnie," he said.

I nodded. I was a little choked up.

"Meeting is back on," he announced.

The lesson here is simple but probably the most important of this entire book: we can talk all day about how we can *see* better, but if our seeing better doesn't translate into *doing* better, then all this conversation is for naught. It helps me to remember that I don't have unlimited time to impact others. With some, I only have a moment. We have to constantly remind ourselves of the preciousness of life. I don't mean that we should live in fear of death. I mean that as leaders we should keep within ourselves a constant sense of urgency where the lives around us are concerned. I have no idea how many more days I have on this planet. I hope I have decades more. In the same way, I have no idea how many days the people I see have left. I've made wrong assumptions before. I assumed my first roommate at Children's had a lifetime ahead of her. She passed away when she was eighteen years old, eighteen months after I met her. I assumed my dad would be around to watch my career at CAT unfold. I envisioned us celebrating the end of my thirty-year career together. He passed away before my career was even half over.

I don't think we ought to go through life with a morbid anxiety inside us. But I do think we need to stop thinking, *I'll go say something to him next time*, or *I'll do that next time I see her.*

It's easy for us to make impact seem so grandiose that we forget we can lift up another person in a single moment, with a smile, a kind word of affirmation, an introduction that conveys, "You matter."

When I met Betty in Uganda, she had ten children with her husband, Henry, whom she'd married at the age of twelve. She had her first baby at fifteen. Over the next twelve years, she gave birth to nine more children. Henry became disabled before the birth of their last two children, who are twins, forcing Betty to take over the daily duties of farming their land. She was twenty-eight years old and strong. Her vision for her children superseded her vision for her own life. In them, she saw her own goals. In her I found strength. I'm glad we met when we did. And I'm glad I saw her.

Betty died of lung cancer in February 2015, two years after I'd met her. Neither of us knew then what little time she had. She was only fifty-six, but there's no doubt she'd aged her body working dusk until dawn on that farm. No vacations. No promotions. Just a dream of providing a better life for her kids.

"A better life" is a common phrase we hear around the topic of poverty. It's easy to downplay the significance of a parent's vision for her children. But for many people living in scarcity, it's the greatest hope of their lives. What a beautiful hope, to hitch your dreams to the life of another.

It's easy for us to make impact seem so grandiose that we forget we can lift up another person in a single moment, with a smile, a kind word of affirmation, an introduction that conveys, "You matter."

When I met her, Betty was a young-looking fifty-four-year-old mother who was working hard to rid her family line of poverty. I couldn't have known how she'd spent the majority of her life—the unique struggles she'd faced and the strength she'd held on to all along the way. But I could see she had a beautiful hope. And I could show her that I saw her.

What we all want—perhaps above all else—is to be seen for all we are and can be, even if we can't see it ourselves. There is no greater gift than to give this insight to another. There is no greater gift than to receive this insight from another. While it's a worthy axiom that those who've been given a lot ought to give a lot, the whole truth is that those who've been given a little can give a lot, too, especially as it relates to the gift of perspective. The Bible story of the widow's mite—where a poor widow gives everything she has—isn't just about money; it's ultimately about the stewardship of our lives.[1] How we see will always dictate how we give. Imagine how the world would improve if we spent as much time looking up to others as we spend looking at ourselves.

Today, Betty's children are working and supporting themselves and their families.

Upon her death, her loans from Opportunity Bank were written off, and the family received money under the bank's insurance policy. Opportunity International met Betty at a point in her life when everyone had looked down on her. Her aspirations for her kids weren't going to be realized, and her family's cycle of poverty was going to continue. Then a small number of people looked up. We saw more than her struggles. We saw her strength and potential, and we entered in. We didn't view her asking for help as a weakness. It was a compelling strength. And it was worthy of our investment.

There are Bettys in all of us.

Can you see it?

Look up and you will.

In his 1989 inaugural address, President George H. W. Bush said:

> I have spoken of a thousand points of light, of all the community organizations that are spread like stars throughout the Nation, doing good. We will work hand in hand, encouraging, sometimes leading, sometimes being led, rewarding. We will work on this in the White House, in the Cabinet agencies. I will go to the people and the

programs that are the brighter points of light, and I will ask every member of my government to become involved. The old ideas are new again because they are not old, they are timeless: duty, sacrifice, commitment, and a patriotism that finds its expression in taking part and pitching in.[2]

Upon taking the presidency, he established the Daily Point of Light Award in 1990 as a way to recognize individuals looking up to others through action. According to the website, the award recognizes "ordinary people who reach beyond themselves to the lives of those in need, bringing hope and opportunity, care and friendship."[3]

In 2018, Don and Joann Tolmie were named Points of Light for their work in establishing and fostering the growth of the Faraja School. Today, one hundred students attend the school full-time. Dozens more have graduated and are extending the legacy of Faraja and the Tolmies. Naming Don and Joann Points of Light is fitting. The title makes me think of a lighthouse on a bluff overlooking the ocean, shining light not on itself but from itself. The lighthouse is there to protect, to serve, to illuminate the path ahead for others. The lighthouse doesn't choose who it will shine its light on—it shines on whoever crosses the path of its bright beam.

Four decades after realizing I was going to be little, I rolled into the Oval Office to discuss an education task force with President Obama. I'd recently been appointed president of the Caterpillar Foundation, and helping eradicate poverty was a primary aim. One of the fundamental pieces of the equation was education. With today's pace of change and the global reach of opportunities, an important aspect of education is enabling students to study abroad and engage with a variety of perspectives, so they can see bigger possibilities in their own lives. One of President Obama's initiatives was a fund called 100,000 Strong, which fuels international partnerships to increase student exchange and training programs.

The program had been in place for a couple of years and was successful, but President Obama wanted to expand it. He asked his staff to invite three corporate representatives whose companies were already funding the initiative to discuss what we thought of it, how it was working, and how it could be grown. I was asked to attend on behalf of Caterpillar.

Besides me and the two other corporate representatives, a small number of university representatives were asked to offer their perspectives too. In total, fifteen of us met at the White House and were escorted to the Roosevelt Room. I was seated at the head of the table—one secret advantage of using a wheelchair and having an immobile neck. For forty minutes, White House representatives hosted a productive conversation. Then the door to the room flew open. I was so deep into the conversation that it startled me. I looked up, and in walked the president.

"Hello, folks!" he exclaimed. "How's it going?"

He went around the table and shook hands with everybody. I was the last one. He came to me and said hello, and I said, "Hi, Mr. President. I'm Michele Sullivan with the Caterpillar Foundation." He shook my hand, and then he hung on to it. "Caterpillar?" he repeated. He is, of course, from Illinois. "You tell everybody at Caterpillar I said hello." I thanked him and said I would.

The president was engaged for nearly an hour. Each

person in the room had a unique viewpoint, but we shared the same vision to improve the lives of underprivileged young people. When we were finishing up, President Obama stood and motioned for us to follow him.

"Let's move into the Oval Office," he said. "We'll wrap this up with a photo."

Chairs slid back and bodies began jockeying for position. I already knew where I was going to stand, so I waited and took up the rear. Once in the Oval Office, I leaned on a couch and covertly enjoyed watching the others time their moves.

Eventually the staff began to position people because no one was committing until the president did. I stood there grinning to myself.

Finally, everybody was in position except me.

"Michele, come over here," the president said. "You're going to stand right here in front of me."

I walked over, and he put his hands on my shoulders. "This is a perfect spot," he whispered. Then the photographer snapped the photo.

There wasn't a partisan prerequisite for being in that room. We had black, white, and brown skin. We were young and old, men and women—even a disabled woman who never rose above four feet in her own shoes.

I get asked a lot if I'm a Democrat or a Republican. People say, "You ran a foundation—you must be a Democrat." Others say, "You were at Caterpillar. Clearly, you're a Republican." How we love to assign labels to each other. It's never the best practice, even if it's a natural inclination. I always say I'm neither a Democrat nor a Republican. I'm a collaborator. That meeting room in the White House was full of collaboration.

I knew not everyone in that room had voted for President Obama. But our agenda wasn't about political dogma. The president holds the most powerful position in the world, but we can all have vision. When we share the same vision, to always look up to one another, we boost life itself.

I know why everyone was jockeying for the right spot in the picture. So do you. We all want to be seen as important.

Believe me, I would have been jockeying for position, too, if I'd thought it might help.

What if we no longer needed to jockey?

What if we believed that we were already seen?

What if we interacted in ways that convey we all have immense value? We all are worthy. It is impossible not to come to this conclusion once you've taken the chance to get to know another person and his or her story.

Seeing, truly seeing, is one of the greatest gifts we can give to one another, especially when society is increasingly placing people in silos. We have to look beyond the surface and be confronted with the truth that there's more to all of us than we can see, and we are more alike than different. Imagine if we began to live this way every day.

When we look up to each other, we will elevate the look of the world.

ACKNOWLEDGMENTS

My goal in this book is to help you see how you are shaped by others and vice versa—for you to truly spot the immense value in everyone, including yourself. Rarely in life do we accomplish things by ourselves. This has certainly held true in all aspects of my life. So many people have influenced and believed in me throughout my journey, directly and indirectly, and this has given me many opportunities and made me who I am today.

Words cannot adequately express my love and gratitude to my family. My parents have always been my biggest supporters. They never wavered as they instilled in me self-esteem and confidence to thrive in a world not necessarily built for someone my size. They surrounded me, and everyone around me, with love. I still work hard every day to be half (no pun intended) the people they are. My gratitude for my older brother and younger sister is just as great. It's not easy being my sibling, yet their support has been steadfast. To this day, my family continues to make memories around the world.

We like to say, "If we have our love for each other and our memories together, what else do we need?"

I greatly appreciate and love all of the people at my kitchen table and in my village. Every day I count my blessings for each and every one of you, whose names would double the size of this book. Many of you have been with me my whole life, and some not so long—this breadth and diversity is what I love the most. I wouldn't be who I am without each one of you shaping me through your words and examples. I think often of all the memories we share, with both tears and laughter.

While this book was a dream of mine, it took a wonderful team to make it a reality. Lucinda Blumenfeld, my literary agent, believed in the book from the start and has guided me brilliantly through the publishing process. Her advice was priceless. My thoughts being turned into passionate stories and lessons would not have been possible without the very talented writer Brent Cole. Brent was by my side through the uplifting stories and the ones I had to write out because I couldn't verbalize them. The HarperCollins Leadership team—Jeff James, Webb Younce, Sara Kendrick, Sicily Axton, Hiram Centeno, Amanda Bauch, and Belinda Bass—brought the book to life in the most amazing way. All of these beautiful people are a part of my village. They have become close friends and counselors as they helped bring my journey to life, with compassion. I've loved all of our laughs and the memories we have made. Thank you for everything you have done.

"Give thanks to the LORD, for he is good;
his love endures forever."
—1 Chronicles 16:34

NOTES

Chapter 2: There Is No Such Thing as Knowledge at First Sight

1. Dr. Martin Luther King Jr., "Conquering Self-Centeredness" (sermon, Dexter Avenue Baptist Church, Montgomery, AL, August 11, 1957), in *The Papers of Martin Luther King, Jr.*, vol 4, *Symbol of the Movement, January 1957–December 1958*, ed. Susan Carson et al. (Berkeley: University of California Press, 1992), 250.

Chapter 3: Seeing Others Takes Sacrifice

1. Jacques Kelly, "Dr. Steven Kopits, 65, Expert on Dwarfism," *Baltimore Sun*, June 19, 2002, http://articles.baltimoresun.com /2002-06-19/news/0206190113_1_dwarfism-kopits-buenos-aires.
2. Kelly.
3. Kelly.
4. Antoine de Saint-Exupéry, *The Little Prince*, trans. Richard Howard (New York: Harcourt, 1943, 2000), 63.

Chapter 6: Make the First Move

1. Dale Carnegie, *How to Win Friends and Influence People*, rev. ed. (New York: Simon and Schuster, 1982), 226.

2. See Proverbs 19:11 NIV.
3. C. S. Lewis, *Mere Christianity*, rev. ed. (New York: HarperSanFrancisco, 2009), 128.

Chapter 7: Asking for Help Is a Strength, Not a Weakness

1. Michael Karson, "The Myth of Independence," *Psychology Today*, December 26, 2013, https://www.psychologytoday .com/us/blog/feeling-our-way/201312/the-myth-independence.
2. Miki Kashtan, "Interdependence in Action," *Psychology Today*, November 30, 2018, https://www.psychologytoday.com/us /blog/acquired-spontaneity/201811/interdependence-in-action.
3. Julie Miller, "The Tragic, Beautiful True Story Behind Peter Dinklage's *My Dinner with Hervé*," *Vanity Fair*, October 19, 2018, https://www.vanityfair.com/hollywood/2018/10 /peter-dinklage-my-dinner-with-herve-villechaize-hbo -fantasy-island.
4. Miller.
5. Frank Wilkins, "The Suicide of Hervé Villechaize—Tattoo," *Reel Reviews*, accessed May 16, 2019, http://reelreviews.com /shorttakes/tattoo/tattoo.htm.

Chapter 10: The Real Measure of Impact

1. See Mark 12:41–44 NIV.
2. George H. W. Bush, inaugural address, January 20, 1989, https://www.bartleby.com/124/pres63.html.
3. Jay Tennier, "Academic Volunteer & Mentor Service Program," Daily Points of Light website, April 18, 2000, https://www.pointsoflight.org/awards/academic-volunteer -mentor-service-program/.

ABOUT THE AUTHOR

Michele Sullivan is the recently retired director of Corporate Social Innovation and president of the Caterpillar Foundation, the philanthropic arm of the multibillion-dollar manufacturing giant Caterpillar, Inc. In addition to her thirty-year career holding various leadership positions at the company, she helped transform the organization into one of the world's most influential corporate foundations, through the launch of its collaborative impact platform known as Together.Stronger.™, a catalyst for shared prosperity that unites businesses, nonprofits, governments, and citizens to combine their strengths to alleviate poverty for millions of people worldwide.

Printed in the USA
CPSIA information can be obtained
at www.ICGtesting.com
CBHW020200251124
17882CB00013B/93